Editor:
Renee Henegar

Editorial Project Manager:
Ina Massler Levin, M.A.

Editor In Chief:
Sharon Coan, M.S.Ed.

Art Direction:
Elayne Roberts

Cover Design:
Darlene Spivak

Product Manager:
Phil Garcia

Imaging:
Hillary Merriman

Cover Artist:
Sue Fullam

Publishers:
Rachelle Cracchiolo, M.S.Ed.
Mary Dupuy Smith, M.S.Ed.

Learning Through Literature
CULTURES
INTERMEDIATE

Author:

Concetta Doti Ryan, M.A.

Illustrator:

Larry Bauer

Teacher Created Materials, Inc.
P.O. Box 1040
Huntington Beach, CA   92647
©1995 Teacher Created Materials, Inc.
Made in U.S.A.
ISBN-1-55734-474-4

Table of Contents

Table of Contents *(cont.)*

Introduction

Learning Through Literature — Cultures is a 144-page resource book which provides specific strategies and activities for integrating middle grade elementary multicultural studies with 34 related children's literature selections. This book addresses current trends in education: multicultural studies and understanding, the whole language movement, and the emphasis on integrating curriculum areas. Educators are making a serious effort to build a society wherein students and people from all different cultures get along. Reading literature by and about those from other cultures helps students to better understand and accept people from those cultures. Using literature in the classroom supports the whole language philosophy which stresses the use of literature to build literacy and create tasks that integrate content areas.

Learning Through Literature: Cultures includes literature selections from the following areas of the world:

Africa
Asia
Caribbean
Central America
Europe
Middle East
North America
South America
South Pacific

Each section contains descriptions of picture books and novels, along with a variety of follow-up activities with supporting projects and pattern pages. An extensive bibliography and map of the area are also provided for each section.

Follow-up activities extend and reinforce both the literature and the cultural concepts by using various forms of expression, including:

Poetry
Writing
Art
Research
Critical Thinking
Dramatics
Group Discussion
Games

The goal of *Learning Through Literature: Cultures* is to improve instruction in the middle grade classrooms by blending multicultural studies and literature, providing hands-on activities that can easily be implemented, and sparking children's interest in other cultures.

A Story, A Story

Author and Illustrator: retold by Gail Haley

Publisher: Macmillan, New York, 1970. 31 pages

Summary: Ananse wants the Sky God's stories to share with his friends. The Sky God, however, makes Ananse prove himself before parting with the valuable stories.

Background Information:

This story is the retelling of an African tale. Its origin is not mentioned in the book.

Connecting Activities:

- Ananse is a popular character of African tales. Challenge students to find and read other stories about Ananse.

- The Sky God asks Ananse for three items before he will share his special stories. Have students write a new story wherein the Sky God asks for three different items. The students should tell the story about how Ananse obtains those new items.

- The people really enjoy the Sky God's stories that Ananse shares with them. Have students write a thank-you letter from any of the villagers to Ananse for his bravery in obtaining the stories.

- In small groups, have students discuss how the Sky God will get new stories now that he has given all his stories to Ananse.

- Have students make a special award for Ananse for the bravery, courage, and intelligence he shows in obtaining the three items for the Sky God. They can use the award form on page 6.

- *A Story, A Story* is an African tale retold by Gail Haley. Ask students how they think Haley's story may be different from the original version.

Ananse's Award

Use the special certificate below to create an award for Ananse to honor his bravery, courage, and intelligence.

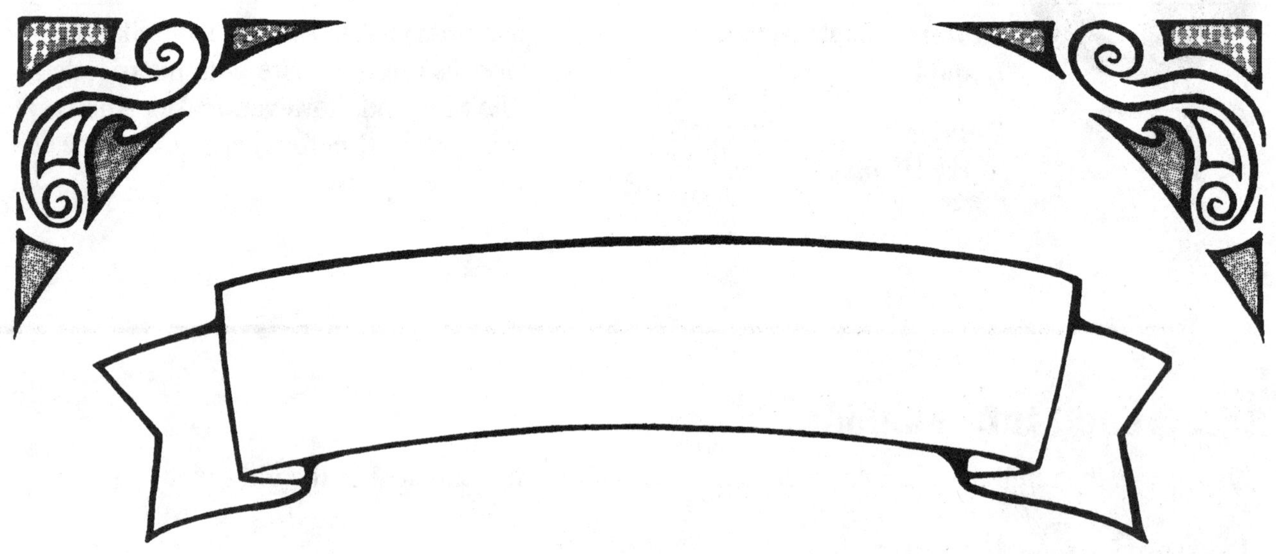

Special Award for:

Because.....

Journey To Jo'burg

Author: Beverly Naidoo

Illustrator: Eric Velasquez

Publisher: Harper Collins, New York, 1986. 75 pages

Summary: Naledi and Tiro journey to South Africa to find their mother because their little sister, Dineo, is very ill.

Background Information on South Africa:

Official Name: Republic of South Africa

Area: 1,221,037 square kilometers

Capitals: Cape Town (legislative), Pretoria (administrative), and Bloemfontein (judicial).

Population: 41,700,000 (1992)

Official Languages: Afrikaans, English

Major Religions: Traditional African religions, Dutch Reformed Church, Anglicanism, Roman Catholicism, Methodism, Hinduism, Judaism

Government: Republic

Monetary Unit: Rand

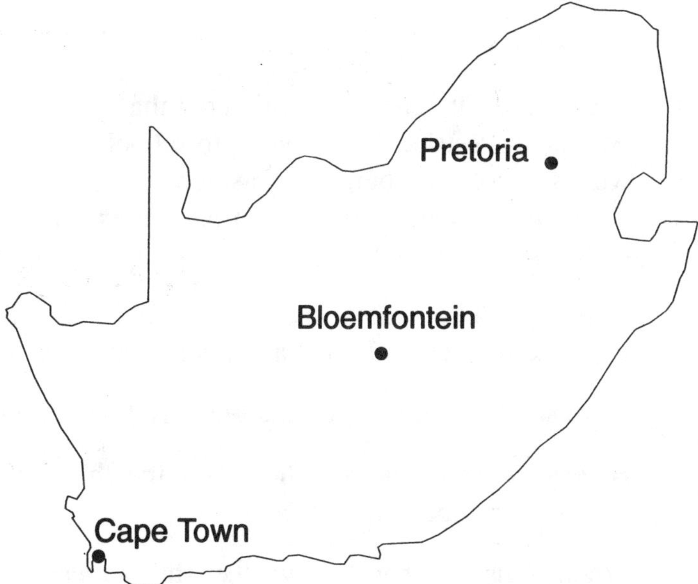

Connecting Activities:

(Chapters 1-3)

- Have students locate South Africa on the Africa map on page 14.

- Naledi wishes she had the money to send her mother a telegram to tell her that Dineo is ill. Imagine that she was able to send the telegram. Have students use telegraphic language to write a telegram to Naledi's mother.

- Students can practice using context clues by making a dictionary of the African terms in the story. Instead of looking up these words in the glossary as they encounter them, ask them to guess the meaning by using the context of the story. They can record their guesses on the activity sheet on page 10. After they have read the entire story, allow students to compare their guesses with the glossary in the back of *Journey to Jo'burg*.

Journey to Jo'burg *(cont.)*

- Have students predict what Nono will do when she finds out that Naledi and Tiro have left to find their mother.

- Naledi and Tiro are afraid they will be put in jail because they do not have a pass to travel. Have students create an application for a pass as they think it would probably be written.

- Naledi and Tiro consider oranges a delicacy. Allow students to enjoy oranges for lunch.

- A young boy offers to help Naledi and Tiro find shelter for the night after he catches them trying to steal oranges. In small groups have students discuss why this boy would want to risk his own safety by helping these children.

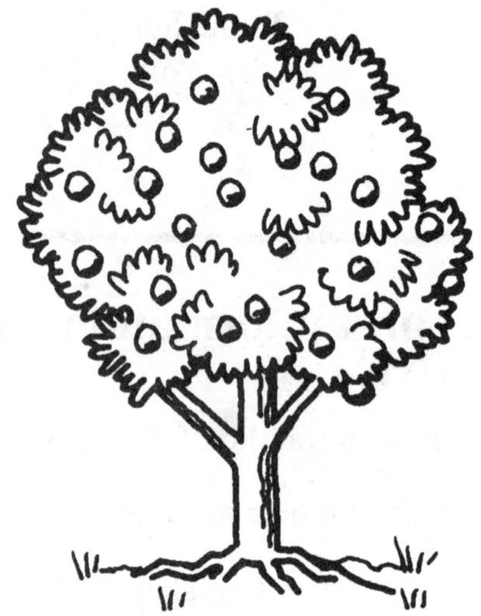

- Have students write a thank you letter to the boy from either Naledi or Tiro for his help.

(Chapters 4-7)

- Naledi and Tiro are upset to find out that Blacks are restricted from going to school with whites in Johannesburg. Have students research apartheid laws that restricted the rights of Blacks in South Africa.

- Naledi and Tiro's mother believes strongly in getting an education. Have students write a lecture from the mother declaring the importance of an education.

- Have students research to find out why Johannesburg is called the "City of Gold."

- Have students predict whether or not the children will be able to find their mother. If they find her, will it be in time to save Dineo?

- When Mma asks her boss whether she can leave to help her sick child, the boss becomes very irritated. The boss sees this as an inconvenience. Have students respond in writing to the attitude of this boss.

- When Mma finally has a moment alone with her children she asks them to tell her their entire story. Have students write the dialogue, and have several students dramatize the scene.

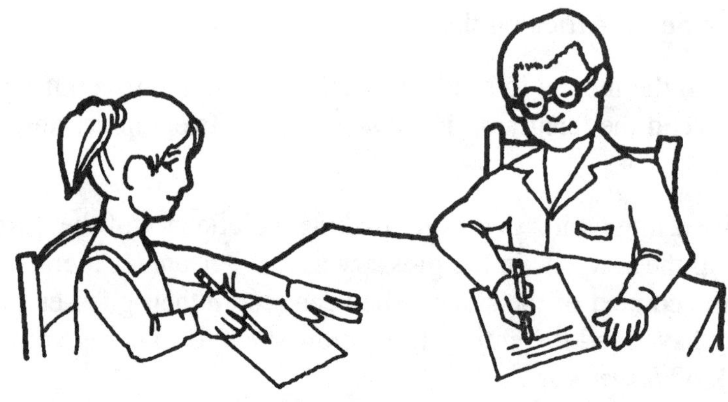

Journey to Jo'burg (cont.)

(Chapters 8-11)

- Grace tells the children about the "Time of Fire." Have students write a news report based on the facts Grace told them about this turbulent time.

- Tiro is anxious to tell Grace what happened to them when they were forced off the train. Have students write Tiro's account of the adventure and then dramatize the monologue for the rest of the class.

- Dumi, a freedom fighter, is away at school. However, he writes to his family and tells them that he will return to fight for freedom. Have students write one of Dumi's letters to his family.

- Naledi begins to wonder what freedom really means. Have students write an essay describing what freedom means to them.

- Grace and Mma have very different opinions about education. Have students debate the importance of education as if they are either Grace or Mma.

- Naledi and Tiro are fascinated by Johannesburg because they have never been to a big city. Have students choose a big city they have never been to and write about what they think it would be like to visit.

(Chapters 12-15)

- Have students write a wish from Naledi hoping that Dineo will become well.

- Naledi wants to continue her friendship with Grace by writing her a letter. Have students write a letter from Naledi to Grace.

- Have students predict whether or not Naledi will become a doctor. If they do not think she will, what is her fate?

- Now that Naledi knows what Blacks in her country face, have students discuss and then write about how her life will change.

- This is a very powerful story about the way Blacks were treated under apartheid. Have students discuss their reactions to the story in small groups. Then ask them to respond to the story in writing. Ask them how it affected them and their lives.

South African Dictionary

As you read the story, you will encounter words from South Africa. Rather than looking these words up in the glossary, try to determine their meanings by using the context of the sentences. Record your definition guess below. When you have finished the book, you can compare your guesses with the glossary in *Journey to Jo'burg*.

Mma ____

Pap ____

Sala sentle _______________________________________

Tsamaya sentle ____________________________________

Rra ____

Baas ____

Awu ____

Tswana ____

Hou jou bek _______________________________________

Mielie ____

Mmangwane ____

How well did you predict the correct definitions?

Sungura and Leopard

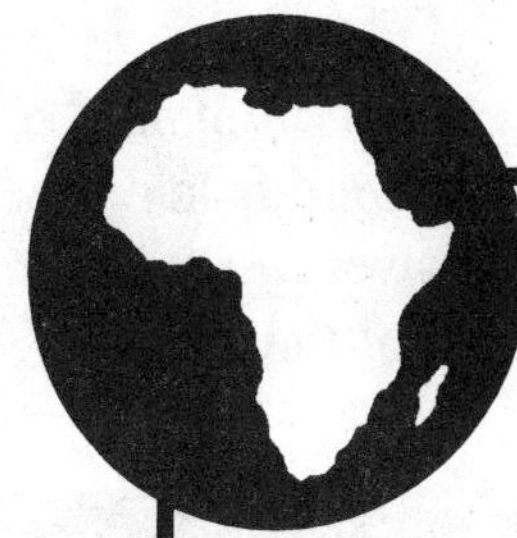

Author and Illustrator: Barbara Knutson

Publisher: Little, Brown and Company, New York, 1993. 23 pages

Summary: When a rabbit and leopard end up sharing the same house, one must go. The rabbit outsmarts the leopard so that he may share the home with his family.

Background Information on Tanzania:

Official Name: United Republic of Tanzania

Area: 945,087 square kilometers

Capital: Dar es Salaam

Population: 27,791,552 (1992)

Official Language: Swahili

Major Religions: Christianity, Islam

Government: Republic

Monetary Unit: Tanzania Shilling

Connecting Activities:

- Have students locate Tanzania on the Africa map on page 14.

- Sungura and the leopard make a beautiful hut with mud and sticks. Allow students to use mud or clay and sticks to make small huts.

- It seems impossible that a rabbit and leopard could live together in peace and harmony. Ask students to write an opinion essay to explain whether or not they think two enemies can live together.

- The story seems to suggest that rabbits are much smarter than leopards. Using the activity sheet on page 12, have students rank the intelligence of the animals according to their own personal ideas. Then, have the students discuss their responses and reasoning with the rest of the class.

- Have students research other Swahili folk tales.

Animal I.Q.

The story seems to suggest that rabbits are much smarter than leopards. Below is a list of animals.
Based on your own personal beliefs, rank the animals in order of intelligence. Rank the animals on a
scale of 1-10, with 1 being the smartest and 10 being the least smart animal. Then answer the questions
at the bottom of the page. Be prepared to share and defend your answers with the rest of the class.

Animal	Ranking
Lion	______________
Dog	______________
Monkey	______________
Cat	______________
Bird	______________
Giraffe	______________
Rhinoceros	______________
Pig	______________
Bear	______________
Alligator	______________

How did you determine which animal was the smartest?

____

____

What criteria did you use to determine intelligence?

____

____

Africa Bibliography

Aardema, Verna. *Bringing the Rain to Kapiti Plain: A Nandi Tale.* (Dial, 1981)

Bryan, Ashley. *Beat the Story-Drum, Pum-Pum.* (Atheneum, 1980)

Bryan, Ashley. *Lion and the Ostrich Chicks, and Other African Folktales.* (Atheneum, 1986)

Climo, Shirley. *The Egyptian Cinderella.* (HarperCollins, 1989)

Diop, Birago. *Mother Crocodile.* (Delacorte, 1981)

Gauch, Patricia Lee. *Noah.* (Philomel, 1994)

Gordon, Sheila. *Waiting for the Rain.* (Bantam, 1987)

Grifalconi, Ann. *Darkness and the Butterfly.* (Little, Brown, 1987)

Haarhoff, Dorian. *Desert December.* (Clarion, 1991)

Heide, Florence Parry & Judith Heide Gilliland. *The Day of Ahmed's Secret.* (Lothrop, Lee, & Shepard, 1990)

Levitin, Sonia. *The Return.* (Atheneum, 1987)

Marie, D. *Tears for Ashan.* (Creative Press Works, 1989)

Myers, Walter Dean. *The Legend of Tarik.* (Viking Press, 1981)

Naidoo, Beverly. *Chain of Fire.* (Lippincott, 1990)

Rochman, Hazel. *Somehow Tenderness Survives: Stories of Southern Africa.* (HarperCollins, 1988)

Stanley, Diane & Peter Vennema. *Shaka: King of the Zulus.* (William Morrow, 1988)

Steptoe, John. *Mufaro's Beautiful Daughters.* (Lothrop, Lee, & Shepard, 1987)

Tadjo, Veronique. *Lord of the Dance.* (Lippincott, 1989)

Walter, Mildred Pitts. *Brother to the Wind.* (Lothrop, Lee & Shepard, 1985)

Weir, Bob and Wendy. *Panther Dream: A Story of the African Rain Forest.* (Hyperion Books, 1991)

Map of Africa

Chin Yu Min and the Ginger Cat

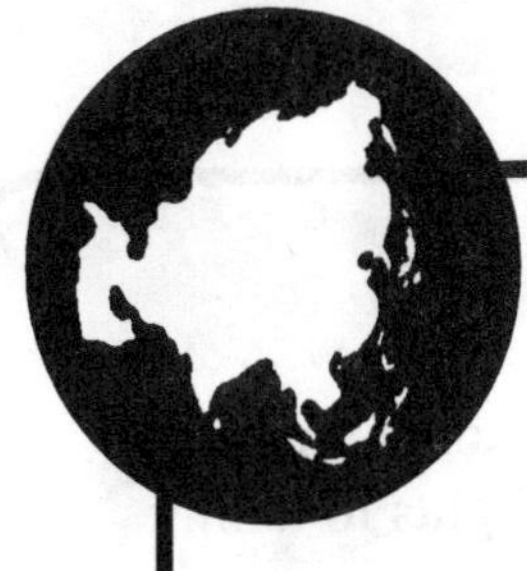

Author: Jennifer Armstrong

Illustrator: Mary Grandpre

Publisher: Crown, New York, 1993. 30 pages

Summary: Chin Yu Min learns a lesson about sharing after her special cat disappears.

Background Information on China:

Official Name: People's Republic of China

Area: 9,562,904 square kilometers

Capital: Beijing

Population: 1,178,500,000 (1993)

Official Language: Mandarin Chinese

Major Religions: Taoism, Buddhism, Islam

Government: Single-party Communist State

Monetary Unit: Yuan

Connecting Activities:

- Have students locate China on the Asia map on page 30.

- It is customary to send a letter of condolence when someone dies. Have students write letters of condolence from neighbors to Chin Yu Min following the death of her husband.

- Have students discuss why Chin Yu Min's neighbors would want to help her when she has always been so mean.

- Chin Yu Min offers the cat free room and board in exchange for all the fish he can catch. Have students imagine that they are the cat's lawyer. How would they advise him about this agreement? Is it fair?

- In small groups, have students discuss why the cat always asks Chin Yu Min what she will do if he goes away.

- After Chin Yu Min finds her cat, she becomes very nice to her neighbors. Have students discuss the lesson she learned.

Grandfather Tang's Story

Author: Ann Tompert

Illustrator: Robert Andrew Parker

Publisher: Crown, New York, 1990. 26 pages

Summary: Using tangram animals, a Chinese grandfather delights in telling stories.

Background Information on China:

See the information provided on page 15.

Connecting Activities:

- Have students locate China on the Asia map on page 30.

- Allow students to have their own tangrams by cutting out the pattern on page 17.

- Challenge students to use their patterns to make all the tangram animals in the story.

- After students have had considerable practice making the tangram animals in the story, challenge them to create an animal on their own with their tangrams. Then have them challenge a friend to make the animal they created.

- Using the tangram animal they created, have students write a story.

- A tangram makes a perfect square. Challenge students to put their tangrams back into perfect squares.

- *Grandfather Tang's Story* is based on the fox fairy characters which are common among Chinese folk tales. Have students research other Chinese folk tales to share with the class.

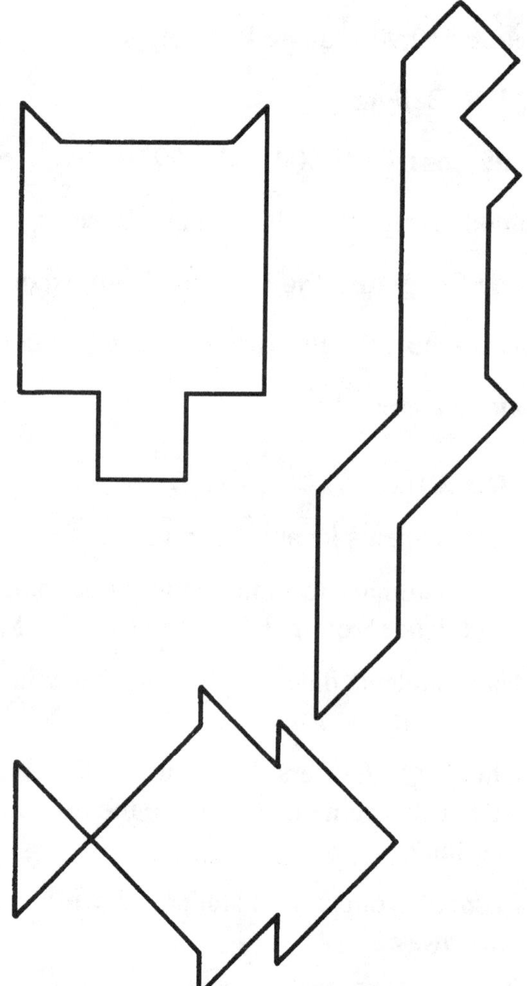

Your Own Tangram

Cut out the tangram pattern below and use it to make the animals in *Grandfather Tang's Story*.

Sadako

Author: Eleanor Coerr

Illustrator: Ed Young

Publisher: Putnam, New York, 1993. 45 pages

Summary: This story is about a Japanese girl, Sadako, and her fight to live after getting leukemia as a result of the dropping of the atom bomb on Hiroshima.

Background Information on Japan:

Official Name: Japan

Area: 377,801 square kilometers

Capital: Tokyo

Population: 124,800,000 (1993)

Official Language: Japanese

Major Religions: Buddhism, Shinto

Government: Constitutional Monarchy

Monetary Unit: Yen

Connecting Activities:

- Have students locate Japan on the Asia map on page 30.

- Sadako considers a blue, cloudless sky a good sign. Have students make a list of American good luck signs.

- Sadako is really excited over the Peace Day celebration. Have students research the significance of Peace Day in Japan.

- Sadako is suffering from leukemia because of the atom bomb the United States dropped on Hiroshima. Have students use the activity sheet on page 20 to research the reasons for and the repercussions of the dropping of the atom bomb.

- Sadako can remember things that happened to her as a baby. Have students write about their earliest childhood memories.

Sadako (cont.)

- Sadako is very excited about the relay race. Allow students to have relay races during their physical education class. You may also allow them to make special ribbons for the winners.

- Sadako begins making paper cranes because according to an old legend if you make 1,000 cranes you will become well. Allow students to make paper cranes by following the directions on page 21. Challenge them to see how many they can make in one, or two, or three weeks. Then, hang these cranes all around the classroom as Sadako did in her hospital room.

- Have students research what leukemia is, how a person contracts it, and how it is treated. Then have them write brief reports of their findings.

- Kenji seems to have little hope. Have students write Kenji a letter to inspire him.

- O Bon is the biggest holiday of the year in Japan. It is a religious observance in which Japanese Buddhists show their respect for loved ones who have passed away. The holiday is celebrated with dance and food. Invite a Japanese Buddhist to come to the class and teach one of the special folk dances. You may also allow students to make traditional Japanese foods such as sushi and teriyaki.

- Following her death, student friends of Sadako wrote letters soliciting donations for her monument. Have students write a letter from one of the students asking for money for the monument and explaining its purpose.

- Have students draw large cranes. Then have them write poetic tributes to Sadako on the cranes. These cranes can be displayed on a bulletin board in the classroom for all to enjoy.

- There is now a statue of Sadako in Hiroshima Peace Park. On Peace Day children hang garlands of paper cranes under the statue. Have students draw pictures of what the statue decorated with cranes may look like and accompany the picture with a news story about the statue and Sadako.

- Have students create a time line of events that led to Sadako's illness and eventual death.

- Challenge students to find poems that would be an appropriate prologue to the story.

World War II

In order to better understand why the United States dropped an atomic bomb on Hiroshima, answer the questions about World War II below. You may need to do some research in order to answer the questions.

1. What countries fought in World War II?

   ____

   ____

2. Which sides were the countries on?

   ____

   ____

3. Why did the United States decide to drop the atomic bomb on Hiroshima?

   ____

   ____

4. Who was president of the United States at the time of the bombing?

   ____

   ____

5. When was the bomb dropped?

   ____

   ____

6. How many people were killed by the atom bomb?

   ____

   ____

7. What happened to the war after the bomb was dropped?

   ____

   ____

8. What park was created in Hiroshima in memory of the bombing?

   ____

   ____

9. What is the current status of Hiroshima?

   ____

   ____

Making Paper Cranes

Sadako tried to make 1,000 paper cranes before her death. You are challenged to make as many paper cranes as you can by following the directions below.

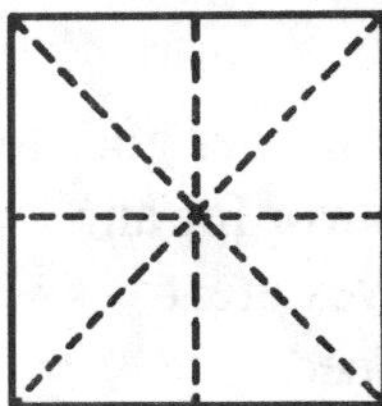

1. Fold an 8" by 8" paper into eighths and then unfold.

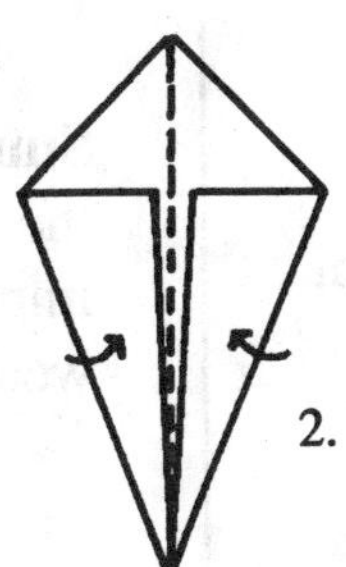

2. Using a diagonal fold as the center, fold the left and right edges into the center line to make a kite shape.

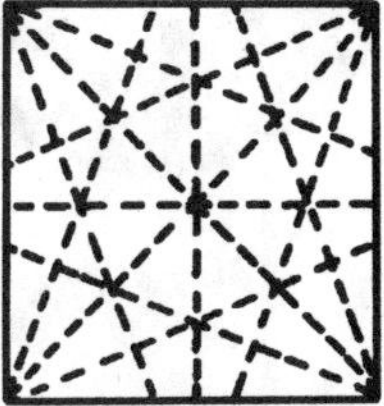

3. Repeat kite fold on each corner. Your opened paper should be creased as shown.

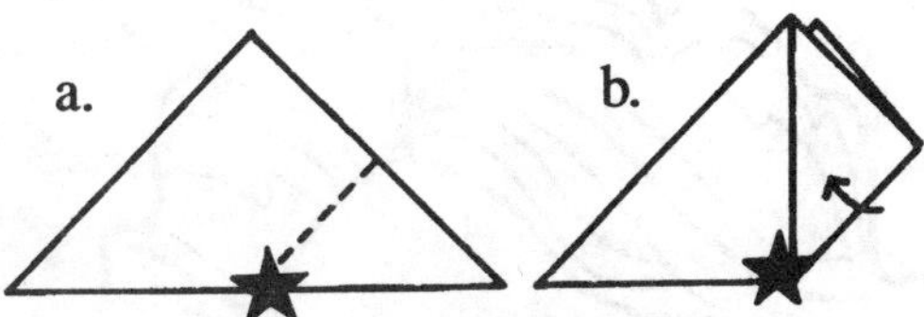

4. Fold the paper in half to make a triangle. Hold it at the star and fold the right side up to meet the top of the triangle.

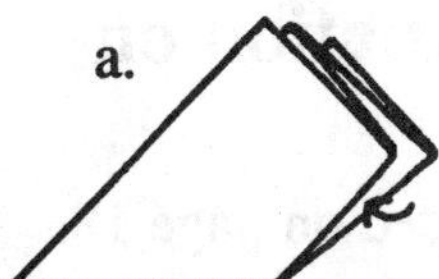

5. Release the fold and make the same fold inside out, with the fold coming between the front and back of the large triangle. Repeat on left side. Sharpen the crease.

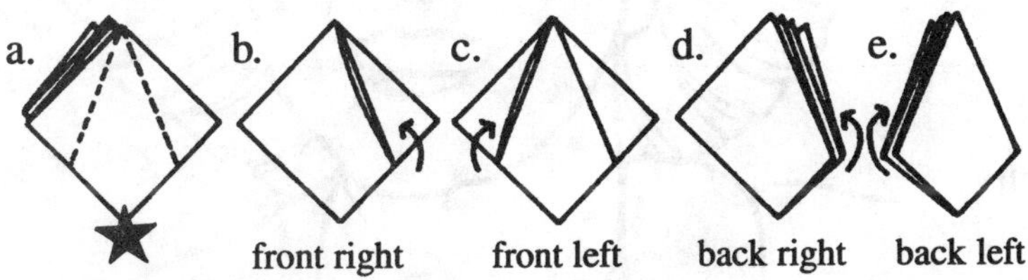

6. Hold the point at the star and fold down the top flap at the broken line. Turn the shape over and repeat the fold on the other side.

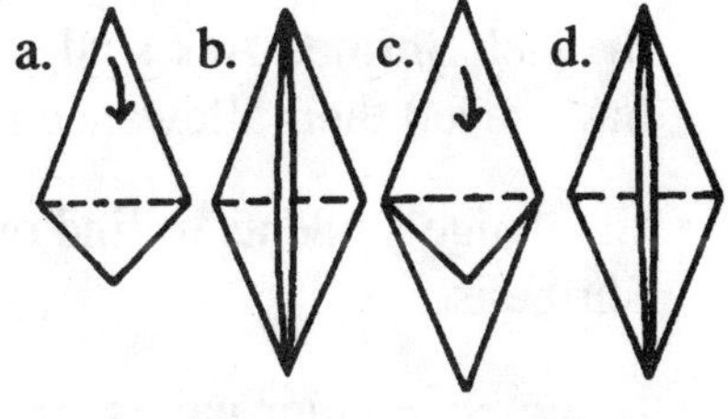

7. Fold down the right flap at the broken line. Release and make the same fold inside out. Repeat on the left side.

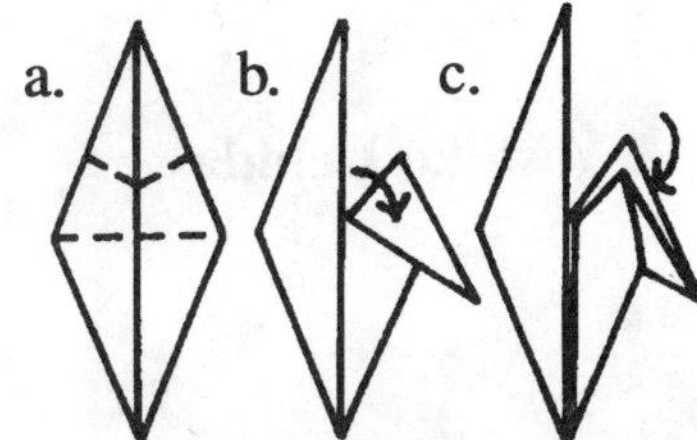

8. Turn the shape as shown and fold the end of the point at the broken line to form the crane's head. Release and make the same fold inside out. Fold down the top flap at the broken line to make a wing. Turn over and fold the other wing.

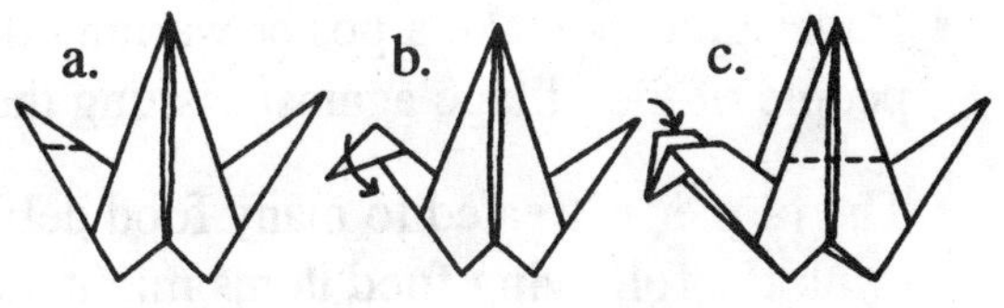

9. Roll the wings around a pencil to give a curved shape.

The Magic Purse

Author: Yoshiko Uchida

Illustrator: Keiko Narahashi

Publisher: Macmillan, New York, 1993. 26 pages

Summary: When a poor farmer goes to the Red Swamp to do a favor for an imprisoned girl, he receives great wealth in return for his deed.

Background Information on Japan:

See the information provided on page 18.

Connecting Activities:

- Have students locate Japan on the Asia map on page 30.

- The farmer was saving his money to visit the Iseh Shrine. Ask students what they have saved their allowance for in the past.

- Challenge students to find out what the Iseh Shrine is.

- Using watercolor paints, have students draw the young girl leaving the swamp to talk to the farmer.

- The girl asks the farmer to deliver a letter to her parents. Have students write what they think the letter says.

Yoshiko Uchida

- Have students make a poster warning the people of the village against visiting the Red Swamp.

- The farmer is treated to many food delicacies by the young girl's parents. Ask students what they think the following food items might taste like: sea bream, fish roe, quail eggs, fried bumblebees, and turtle chowder.

- Yoshika Uchida is a popular author. Have students read one of her other books such as: *Journey Home, A Jar of Dreams,* or *The Best Bad Thing.*

The Clay Marble

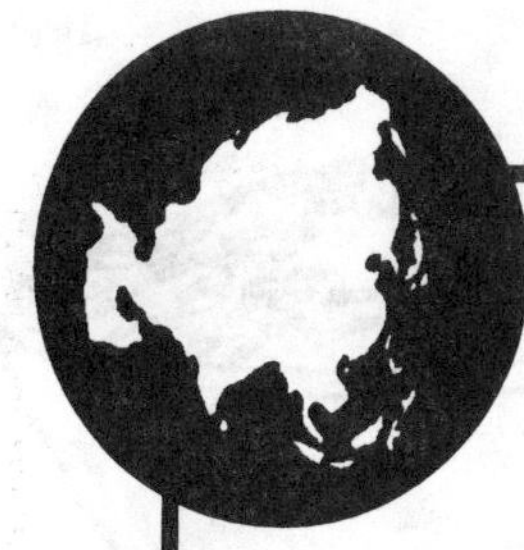

Author: Minfong Ho

Publisher: Farrar, Straus, & Giroux, New York, 1991. 160 pages

Summary: Dara and her family try to survive after their home in Cambodia is bombed. They live in a refugee camp on the Cambodia-Thailand border until they can safely return to their homeland.

Background Information on Cambodia:

Official Name: Cambodia (Kampuchea)

Area: 181,035 square kilometers

Capital: Phnom Penh

Population: 9,000,000 (1993)

Official Language: Khmer

Major Religion: Buddhism

Government: Constitutional Monarchy

Monetary Unit: New Riel

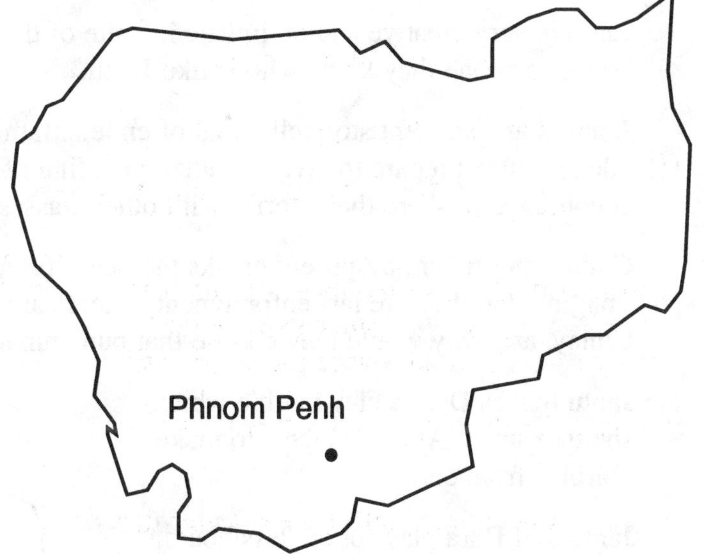

Connecting Activities:

(Chapters 1-3)

• Have students locate Cambodia on the Asia map on page 30.

• In order to better understand the story, have students research what the war in Cambodia was all about.

• Dara mentions that one night her father was killed. Have students predict why the government would want her father to be killed.

• When Dara's family meets Nea and her family, Nea offers to feed them. Sarun refuses the rice Nea offers him. Have students discuss why Sarun would refuse the food when he is so hungry.

• After the students have researched the war in Cambodia, ask them who they think is providing the food on the lunch truck for the children.

The Clay Marble (cont.)

- Dara savors every grain of the rice Nea gives her because she is so hungry. She describes the rice in great detail in the book. Allow students to eat rice and then write a sensory descriptive piece describing what the rice looked like, smelled like, tasted like, and felt like.

- Dara and Jantu notice a woman at the lunch truck who is writing in a notebook. Ask students who they think the lady is. Then, have them write a page as if they are the lady the girls see.

(Chapters 4-6)

- Have students predict what will happen to the relationship of Nea and Sarun in the future. Will they get together?

- The Cambodians talk a great deal about the monsoons. Have students research what monsoons are and how often they occur in Cambodia.

- Jantu is very creative and optimistic in spite of the tragedy she has overcome. Have students write about someone they know who is like Jantu.

- Jantu is an excellent storyteller and often tells famous folk tales. Have students find a favorite folk tale and then prepare to give a dramatic reading of the folk tale to the class. Students may also be encouraged to share their stories with other classes.

- Chnay, an orphan, purposely breaks the beautiful toy that Jantu made for Dara. Have students imagine that they are law enforcement officers at the camp. What punishment would they assign to Chnay, and why would they choose that punishment?

- Jantu makes Dara a clay marble which she treasures. Allow students to make marbles from clay.

- Jantu and Dara play for endless hours with the little clay figures that Jantu made. Allow students to make several clay figures of any characters they choose from the story. Then, have them make a diorama background of the refugee camp to place the clay figures in for display.

- Jantu and Dara debate what they think a "real family" is. Have a class debate on this same issue.

The Clay Marble (cont.)

- Jantu recalls eating mangos and how much she loved them. Allow students to try either mangos, guavas, or papayas, all of which are mentioned in the story. Then, take a class vote on which fruits the students like the best.

(Chapters 7-10)

- To Dara the concept of "fighting for peace" does not make sense. Ask students to write an essay explaining what to "fight for peace" may mean. Also ask them to include their opinion about what is worth going to war over.

- Dara tells Jantu a story about how she is afraid of thunder. She explains how when her father was alive he would comfort her and make her less afraid. Have students write about a special memory they have of a relative comforting them.

- Have students predict what is going to happen to the Cambodians after the bomb is dropped.

- Have students predict whether or not Baby will survive his complications from the bomb.

- Have students discuss in small groups what they think Dara's family must be going through once they realize that Dara, Jantu, and Baby are missing.

- After the many times Chnay has been mean to Dara, he suddenly offers to help her find her family. Is he really the bully everyone thinks he is? Have students write essays about what they think the "real" Chnay is like.

(Chapters 11-14)

- Dara gains the strength and courage to stand up to the soldier regarding the food she took and eventually asks him for a job. She thinks she is able to do this because of the "magic" marble. Have students discuss as a class how Dara found the strength and courage. Was it the marble or something else?

- Using the portrait frame on page 27 have students draw a picture of Dara's family for Chnay to use as he helps Dara search for them.

The Clay Marble *(cont.)*

- Have students write the conversation that may have occurred between Dara and her mother as they are reunited.

- Have students predict what will happen to Chnay now that Dara has found her family.

- In small groups, have students discuss why Chnay left instead of staying with Dara and her family.

- Sarun and Dara have changed greatly since the bombing. Have students use the activity sheet on page 28 to record and analyze the changes in these two main characters.

- Discuss the term "foreshadow" with students. Then discuss the line, "nothing can hold us back now." What does this line suggest may happen?

- Jantu has a rough time in the hospital alone with Baby. Have students write three diary entries for Jantu, describing her experiences and the people she met.

(Chapters 15-18)

- Imagine that Dara could say anything she wants to Sarun. Have students dramatize what these two main characters would say to each other about Sarun becoming so involved in the army.

- Dara is devastated by the death of Jantu. Have students write a poetic tribute to Jantu from Dara.

- Have students write a different final chapter to the story, imagining that Sarun refuses to return to Cambodia with the family.

- Have students imagine that *The Clay Marble* is going to be made into a movie. Ask them which movie stars they would cast as each character and why. Then, ask them to create a new title and create a movie poster advertisement for the movie.

- Have students imagine that Dara is about to be granted three wishes. Have them write about what those three wishes would be and why she would choose them.

- Have students write an essay describing the ways in which the story affected them.

- Have students research what life is like in Cambodia today.

Family Portrait

Draw a picture of Dara's family to help Chnay in his search for them.

Character Analysis

After the bombing Sarun and Dara's characters really change. Make notes describing their characters before and after the bombing. Then, analyze what you believe to be the most significant change of all.

Sarun

Before	After

Dara

Before	After

1. What do you think is the most significant change in Sarun's personality and why?

   ____

   ____

   ____

2. What do you think is the most significant change in Dara's personality and why?

   ____

   ____

   ____

Asia Bibliography

Bang, Molly Garrett. *Tye May and the Magic Brush.* (Greenwillow, 1981)

Choi, Sook Nyul. *Echoes of the White Giraffe.* (Houghton Mifflin, 1993)

Choi, Sook Nyul. *Year of Impossible Goodbyes.* (Houghton Mifflin, 1991)

Ginsburg, Mirra. *The Chinese Mirror: A Korean Folktale.* (Harcourt, 1988)

Haskins, Jim. *Count Your Way Through China.* (Carolrhoda, 1987)

He, Liyi. *The Spring of Butterflies and Other Folktales of China's Minority Peoples.* (Lothrop, Lee, & Shepard, 1987)

Ho, Minfong. *Rice Without Rain.* (Lothrop, Lee, & Shepard, 1990)

Kipling, Rudyard. *Kim.* (Puffin, 1991)

Lawson, Julie. *The Dragon's Pearl.* (Clarion, 1993)

Leaf, Margaret. *Eyes of the Dragon.* (Lothrop, Lee, & Shepard, 1987)

Lee, Jeanne M. *Toad Is the Uncle of Heaven: A Vietnamese Folktale.* (Holt, 1985)

Lewis, Elizabeth Foreman. *Young Fu of the Upper Yangtze.* (Bantam, 1960)

Namioka, Lensey. *Island of Ogres.* (Harper & Row, 1989)

Otsuka, Yuzo. *Suho and the White Horse: A Legend of Mongolia.* (Viking, 1982)

Say, Allen. *Grandfather's Journey.* (Houghton Mifflin, 1993)

Snyder, Dianne. *The Boy of the Three-Year Nap.* (Houghton Mifflin, 1988)

Watkins, Yoko Kawashima. *So Far from the Bamboo Grove.* (Lothrop, Lee, & Shepard, 1986)

Wilson, Barbara Ker. *Wishbones.* (Macmillan, 1993)

Map of Asia

RUSSIA
Perm
Sverdlovsk
Tyumen
Tomsk
Krasnoyarsk
Kansk
Bratsk
Bodaybo
Aldan
Omsk
Novosibirsk
Abakan
Sea of Okhotsk
Petropavlovsk
Okha
Kustanay
Pavlodar
Biysk
Irkutsk
Skovorodino
Aktyubinsk
Temir Tau
Semipalatinsk
Zyryanovsk
Altay
Petrovsk
Zabaykalskiy
Chita
Baley
Qiqian
Svobodnyy
Blagoveshchensk
Komsomol'sk
Chelkar
Karaganda
Jirgalanta
Jibhalanta
Ulaan Baator
Ondor Haan
Hailar
Khabarovsk
KAZAKHSTAN
Aralsk
Balkhash
MONGOLIA
Ongin
Qiqihar
Yuzhno Sakhalinsk
Kzyl Orda
Sayr Usa
Harbin
UZBEKISTAN
Tashkent
KYRGYZSTAN
Urumqi
Hamie
Baotou
Changchun
Jilin
Vladivostok
Sapporo
TURKMENISTAN
Kuqa
Yumen
Jiuquan
Shenyang
NORTH KOREA
Sea of Japan
Ashkhabad
Dushanbe
TAJIKISTAN
Shache
Qiemo
Xining
Yinchuan
Lanzhou
Taiyuan
Qingdao
Pyongyang
SOUTH KOREA
Seoul
JAPAN
Osaka
Tokyo
Mashhad
Khotan
X'ian
Shanghai
East
China Sea
IRAN
Herat
Kabol
Srinagar
CHINA
Qamdo
Chengdu
Chongqing
Wuhan
AFGHANISTAN
Islamabad
Lahore
Gar
Lhasa
Changsha
Fuzhou
Pacific
Ocean
Qandahar
Zahedan
New Delhi
NEPAL
Kathmandu
BHUTAN
Guiyang
Taipei
TAIWAN
PAKISTAN
INDIA
Kanpur
Varanasi
BANGLADESH
Dacca
Guangzhou
Victoria
HONG KONG
Karachi
Ahmadabad
Calcutta
Mandalay
VIETNAM
Hanoi
Nagpur
MYANMAR
LAOS
Haikou
Philippine Sea
Bombay
Vishakhapatnam
Yangon
Vientiane
Arabian Sea
Hyderabad
Panaji
Bay of Bengal
THAILAND
Bangkok
South
China
Sea
Manila
PHILIPPINES
Madras
Kozhikoda
KAMPUCHEA
Da Nang
Phnom Penh
Saigon
Colombo
SRI LANKA
Davao
MALAYSIA
Kuala Lumpur
Singapore
SINGAPORE
BRUNEI
MALAYSIA
Manado
Indian Ocean
Pakfak
Jayapura
Wowak
Amtion
PAPUA
NEW GUINEA
Jakarta
Ujungpandung
INDONESIA
Daru
Port Moresby
Kupang
Coral Sea
Darwin
Wyndham
Daly Waters
Cairns
Derby
Townsville
1000 Km
1000 Mi.
AUSTRALIA
Onslow
Alice Springs
Rockhampton

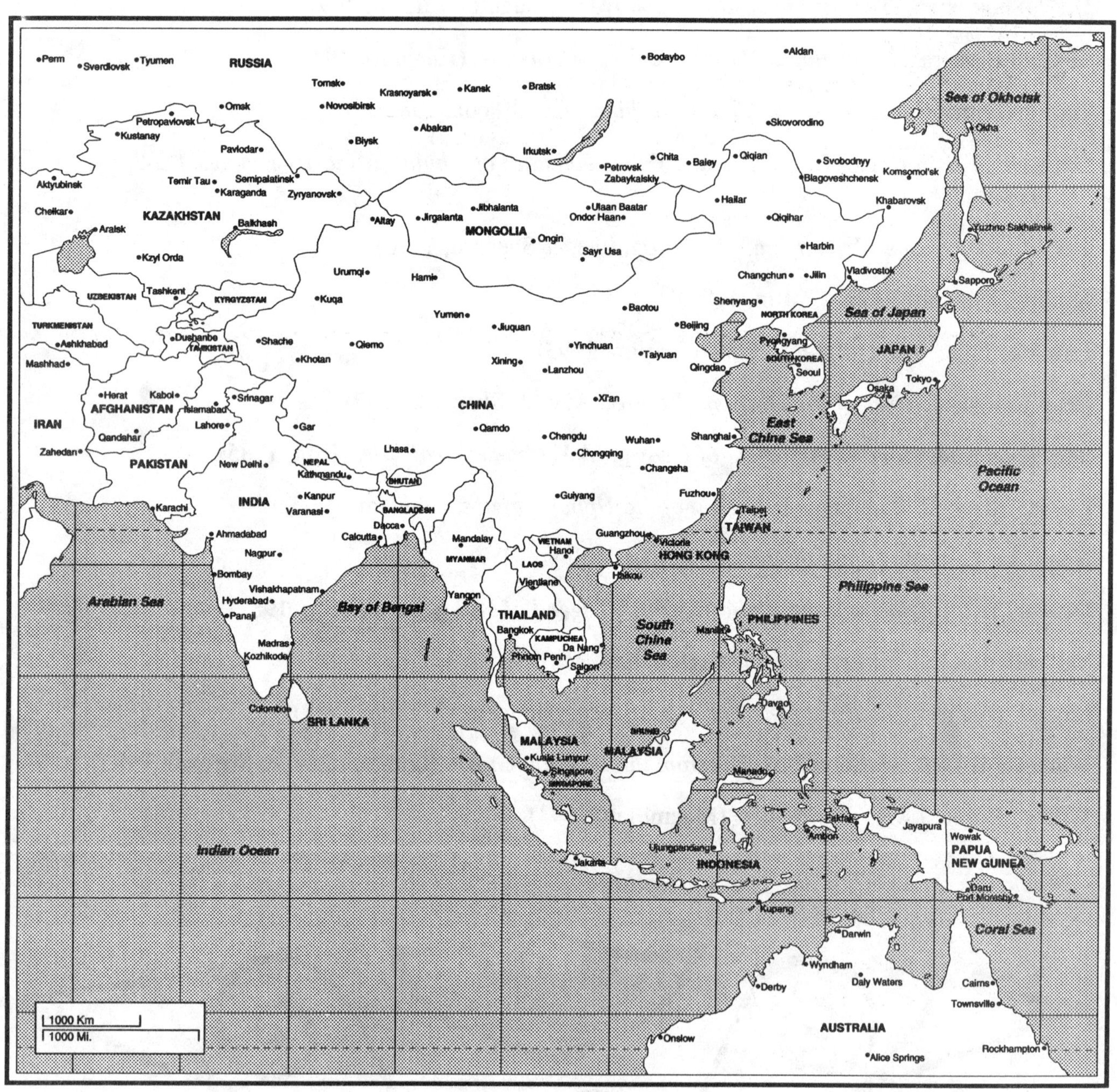

The Jolly Mon

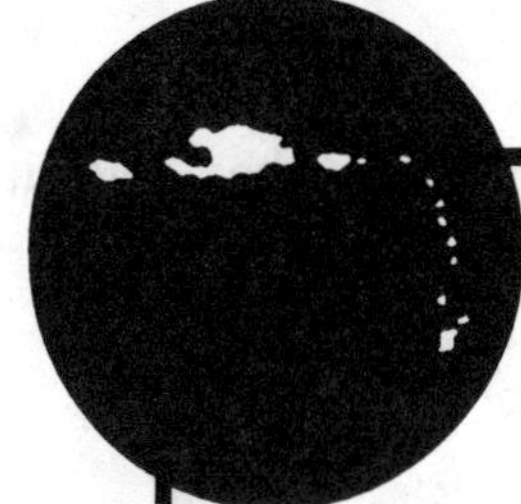

Author: Jimmy Buffett & Savannah Jane Buffett

Illustrator: Lambert Davis

Publisher: Harcourt, San Diego, 1988. 26 pages

Summary: A fisherman from Bananaland entertains the island residents with his beautiful music.

Background Information:

The story takes place on a fictitious island in the Caribbean, Bananaland.

Connecting Activities:

- Ask students how they think the Jolly Mon got his special name.

- The Jolly Mon enjoys looking at the stars. Have students research the Orion constellation, the stars that help guide the Jolly Mon in his travels.

- The Jolly Mon finds a guitar with a golden inscription on it. Have students analyze what this inscription may mean.

- One day while the Jolly Mon is traveling, he receives word that the King of Bananaland has died. Have students write letters from the princess to the Jolly Mon, asking him to return to cheer up the people of Bananaland.

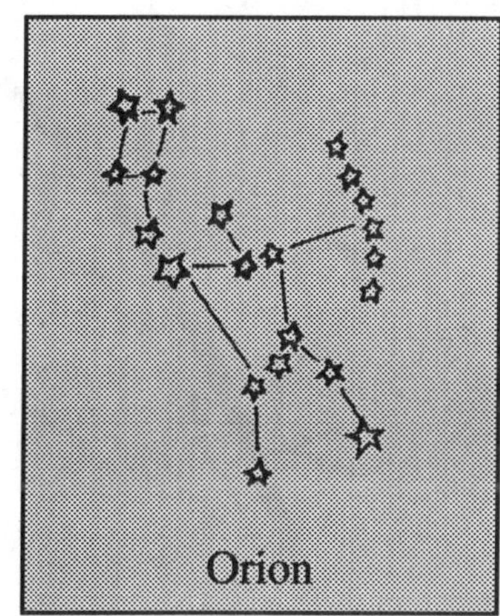

Orion

- The dolphin that saves the Jolly Mon is named Albion. Have students research to find out if there is any special meaning to this name.

- Have students write poems or songs from the Jolly Mon to the dolphin for saving his life. They can write poems or songs on the dolphin pattern on page 32.

- Allow students to sing the Jolly Mon song found at the end of the book called "Jolly Mon Sing" by Jimmy Buffett.

Albion, A Special Dolphin

Albion saved the Jolly Mon's life. As a tribute to this special dolphin, write a poem or song for him from the Jolly Mon. You can write your special poem or song in the dolphin pattern below, then color it.

Timothy of the Cay

Author: Theodore Taylor

Publisher: Harcourt, San Diego, 1993. 163 pages

Summary: This is a prequel/sequel to the classic story *The Cay* written by Taylor over twenty years ago. It tells the story of Timothy prior to (prequel) his adventure with Phillip at the Cay and Phillip's story after (sequel) their adventure at the Cay.

Background Information on St. Thomas:

St. Thomas is one of seven main islands that make up the Virgin Islands. St. Thomas, St. Croix, and St. John all belong to the United States. The other four islands belong to the United Kingdom. The total area of the three islands belonging to the United States, is 495 square kilometers. The population is 101,809 as of 1990. The capital of the three islands is Charlotte Amalie, which is located on St. Thomas.

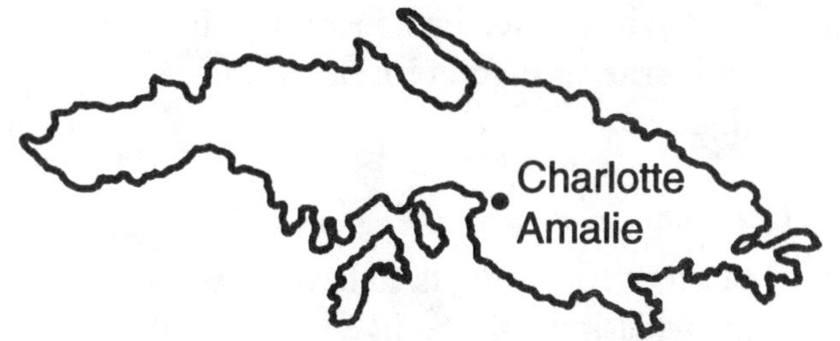

Connecting Activities:

(Chapters 1-2)

- News of Phillip's safe return begins to spread like wildfire. Have students create an interview sheet of questions to ask Phillip about his adventure. Then pair students and have them ask each other the interview questions, posing as an interviewer from a newspaper and as Phillip. Finally, have them create news reports based on the answers they received.

- Have students create dispatch announcements similar to the example on page one of *Timothy of the Cay,* reporting on Phillip's condition.

- Imagine that Phillip's parents do not yet know that he has been safely rescued. Have students create a "missing" poster announcing Phillip's disappearance.

Timothy of the Cay *(cont.)*

- Have students find out what a "cay" is.

- Discuss with the class the way in which the book is structured, alternating between the prequel and the sequel. Make sure students understand both of these terms.

- There are many points in the story where it will be helpful to know the parts of a sailboat. Using the activity sheet on page 38, have students label the parts of a sailboat.

- Have students predict what Tante Hannah will say about Timothy's job on the boat.

- There are often hurricanes in St. Thomas. Several years ago there was a devastating hurricane that hit St. Thomas and several other Caribbean islands. Have students research this hurricane and its effects and write research reports of their findings.

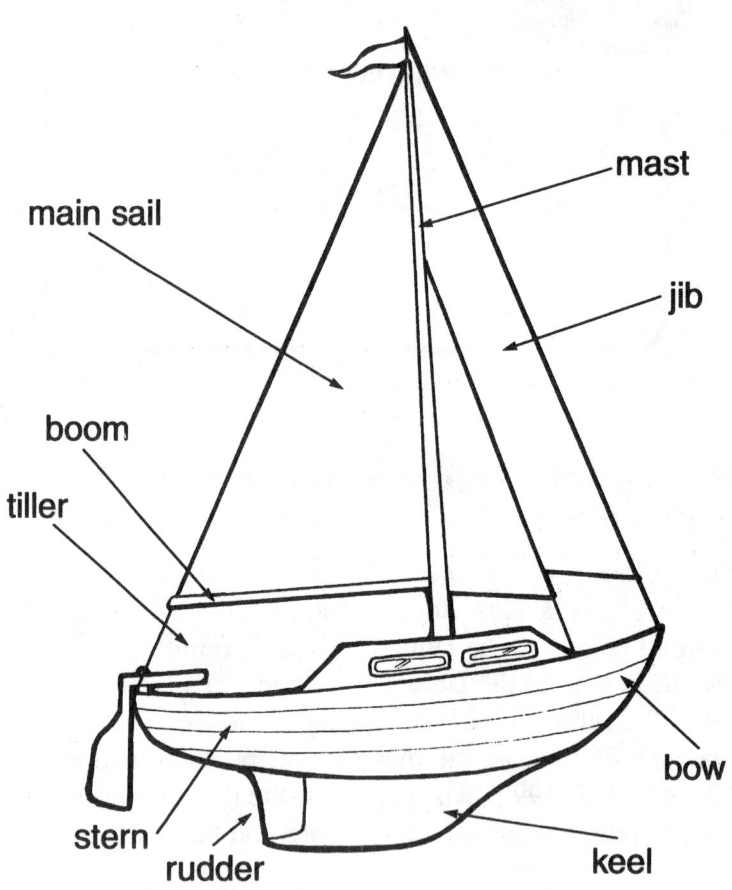

(Chapters 3-5)

- In order for students to have a feel for what it would be like to be blind, have them participate in this experiential activity. Pair students and have one use a blindfold for half the day while being guided by the partner. At the midpoint of the day, have students switch places so both partners have the "blind" experience.

- Timothy was abandoned by his parents on a doorstep. He was raised by the occupant of the house, Tante Hannah. Have students predict what happened to Timothy's parents and what they were like.

- Have students respond to the quote "Wisdom rarely comes from books."

- In small groups, have students discuss who they think will have a more difficult time dealing with Timothy's departure, Phillip or Tante Hannah.

- Have students write an essay describing what it must have been like for Phillip to suddenly go blind.

Timothy of the Cay (cont.)

(Chapters 6-8)

- In St. Thomas residents have to be careful of scorpions. Have students research the dangers of scorpions and draw pictures of them. Perhaps someone from a local pet store can be convinced to bring a scorpion to your classroom for the students to see.

- Marbles are a popular game among the children in St. Thomas. Allow students to play marble games.

- Timothy worries about being homesick while on the boat for so long. Have students draw pictures of St. Thomas and Tante Hannah to help Timothy remember them during his long voyage.

- Timothy can barely contain his excitement about his new job aboard a ship. When he learns that the ship has sailed without him his disappointment is almost unbearable. Have students write letters of advice to Timothy, offering suggestions to him on how to deal with such disappointment.

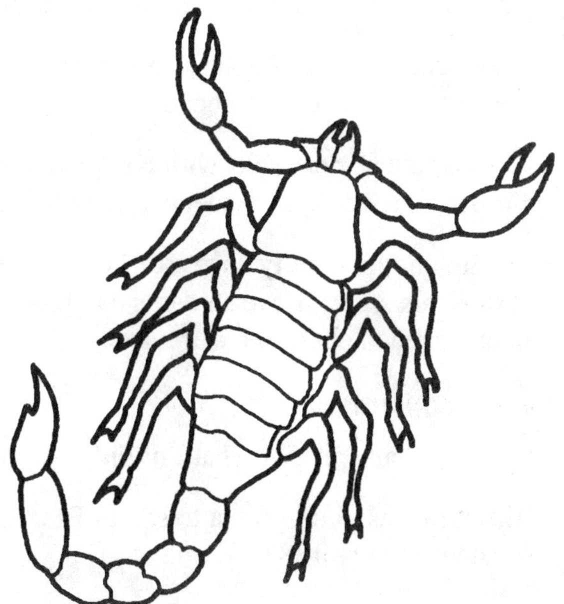

- Phillip has many strong memories about his time spent with Timothy on the cay. Have students write descriptive essays about the experience at the cay while listening to a tape of ocean sounds. These "environmental" tapes can be found in most record stores.

- Challenge students to read *Robinson Crusoe* and compare that story to Phillip's experience.

- The ship Timothy was on went to the Grain Coast, the Gold Coast, and the Ivory Coast. Have students locate all three places on the Africa map on page 14.

- Have students research slavery and emancipation in St. Thomas and St. Croix.

(Chapters 9-12)

- Have students predict Phillip's chances of being able to see again.

- Phillip wants to go back to the cay, which his mother does not understand at all. She told him that it made no sense. Have students discuss in small groups a time when they wanted to do something that others may have thought did not make sense.

Timothy of the Cay (cont.)

- Phillip's mother does not seem to appreciate what Timothy did for her son on the cay. Have students write an opinion essay describing what they think of Phillip's mother's attitude.

- Have students respond to the following quote, "Under the skin we are all the same."

- Many people in St. Thomas believe the obeah has special powers. As a class discuss whether or not students believe in this obeah.

- Phillip's doctor explains with complete candor all the risks and procedures of the surgery to correct Phillip's vision. Ask students if they think this was an appropriate way to handle a young patient.

- Phillip and his family have a difficult decision to make regarding his life-threatening surgery to restore his sight. Have students complete the decision tree located on page 39 to predict what decision each character will make.

(Chapters 13-16)

- Have students predict what Phillip's fate will be and how the operation will go.

- Timothy was going to sea to sail to Brazil. Have students locate Brazil on the South America map located on page 138.

- It was very challenging for Timothy to overcome his fear of climbing high to reach the sails on the boat. Have students write about a time they overcame a fear.

- Phillip is amazingly calm the night before his operation. Have students write a diary entry for Phillip the night before the surgery, explaining his thoughts and describing any final requests he may have. Also, have students include a message to Phillip's parents in case he does not survive the surgery.

- Have students discuss why Luther made Timothy climb back up the ropes to the sails when it clearly was not necessary for him to do so.

(Chapters 17-20)

- Have students discuss what they think Timothy would say to Phillip if he could be there right before Phillip's surgery.

Timothy of the Cay *(cont.)*

- Timothy begins thinking about the fact that he is getting old and has never taken a wife. Have students create a list of qualities they think Timothy would want in a wife.

- Have students write poems as tributes to Tante Hannah's life and what she did for Timothy. Then have them illustrate the poems.

- Timothy's lifelong dream is to own his own boat and be the captain. Have students write essays about their own personal dreams.

- When Timothy finally buys his own boat, he starts a transport business. Have students create an ad for Timothy's new business.

(Chapters 21-23)

- While Phillip is recovering his parents read to him to cheer him up. As a class, have students create a list of books they would read to Phillip to cheer him up.

- In small groups, have students discuss whether or not they would like to be sailors.

- Have students discuss why they think Phillip continues to see and talk to Timothy. Is there something wrong with him?

(Chapters 24-27)

- Allow students to play dominoes, a popular game in St. Thomas.

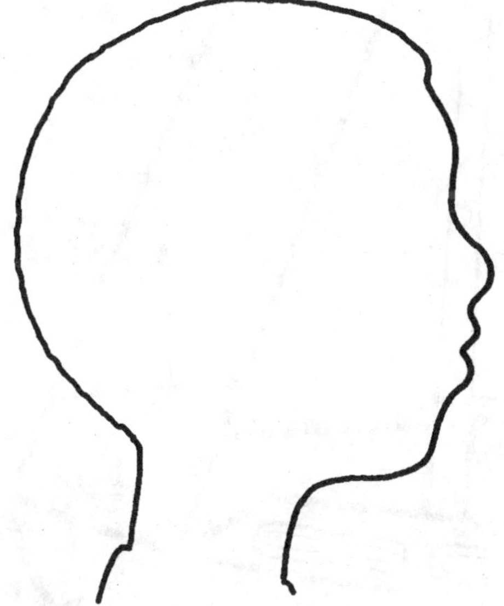 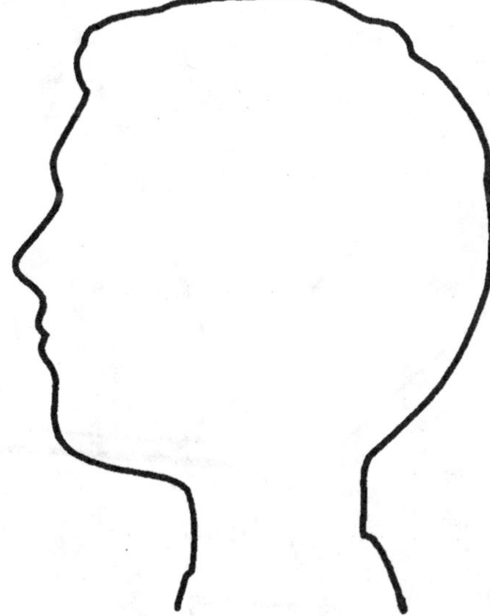

- Have students create a contrast chart to help them discuss the differences between being intelligent and being wise.

- When Phillip has recovered from his surgery his father takes him back to see the cay. Have students write a diary entry for Phillip describing what it is like to return to the cay.

- Using the silhouettes on page 40, have students write a detailed description of the personalities of both Timothy and Phillip. Then have them discuss how they are alike and different.

Knowing a Sailboat

Timothy is constantly talking about the parts of a sailboat in the book. Research the parts of a sailboat, then use the terms to label the picture below. Keep this picture handy while reading *Timothy of the Cay.*

Sailboat Terms: mast, jib, keel, mainsail, tiller, bow, stern, rudder, boom

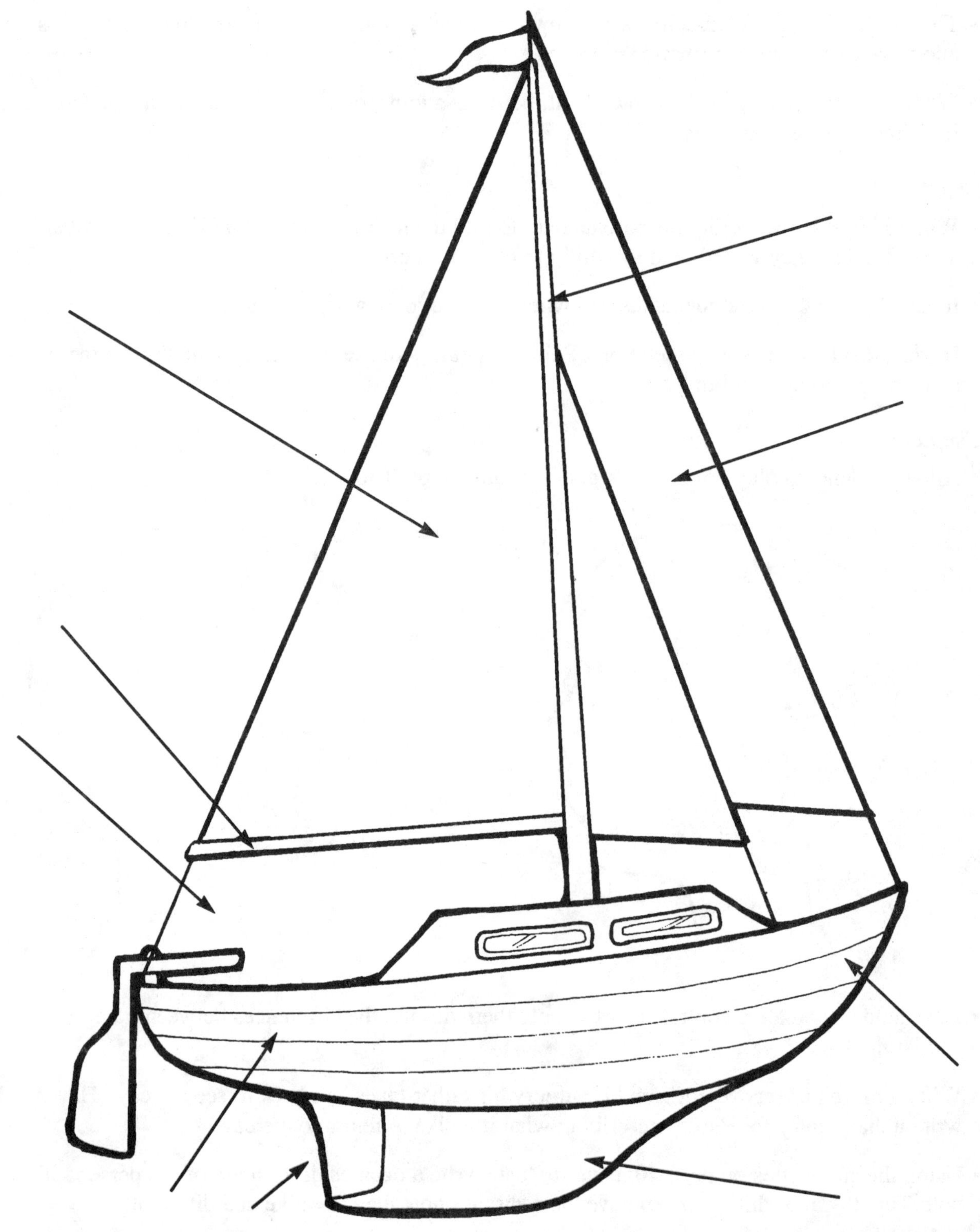

Decision Tree

Phillip and his family have a most difficult decision to make regarding the surgery to possibly correct his vision. Fortunately, the doctor is frank with the family regarding the pros and cons of the surgery. List all the pros and cons below. Then complete the decision tree noting what decision you think each of the three characters will make regarding the surgery.

Pros	**Cons**
______________	______________
______________	______________
______________	______________
______________	______________
______________	______________

Decision Tree

Mom

Dad

Phillip

Personality Profiles

You learned a great deal about the personalities of both Timothy and Phillip as you read *Timothy of the Cay*. In the silhouettes below, write a detailed description of each character.

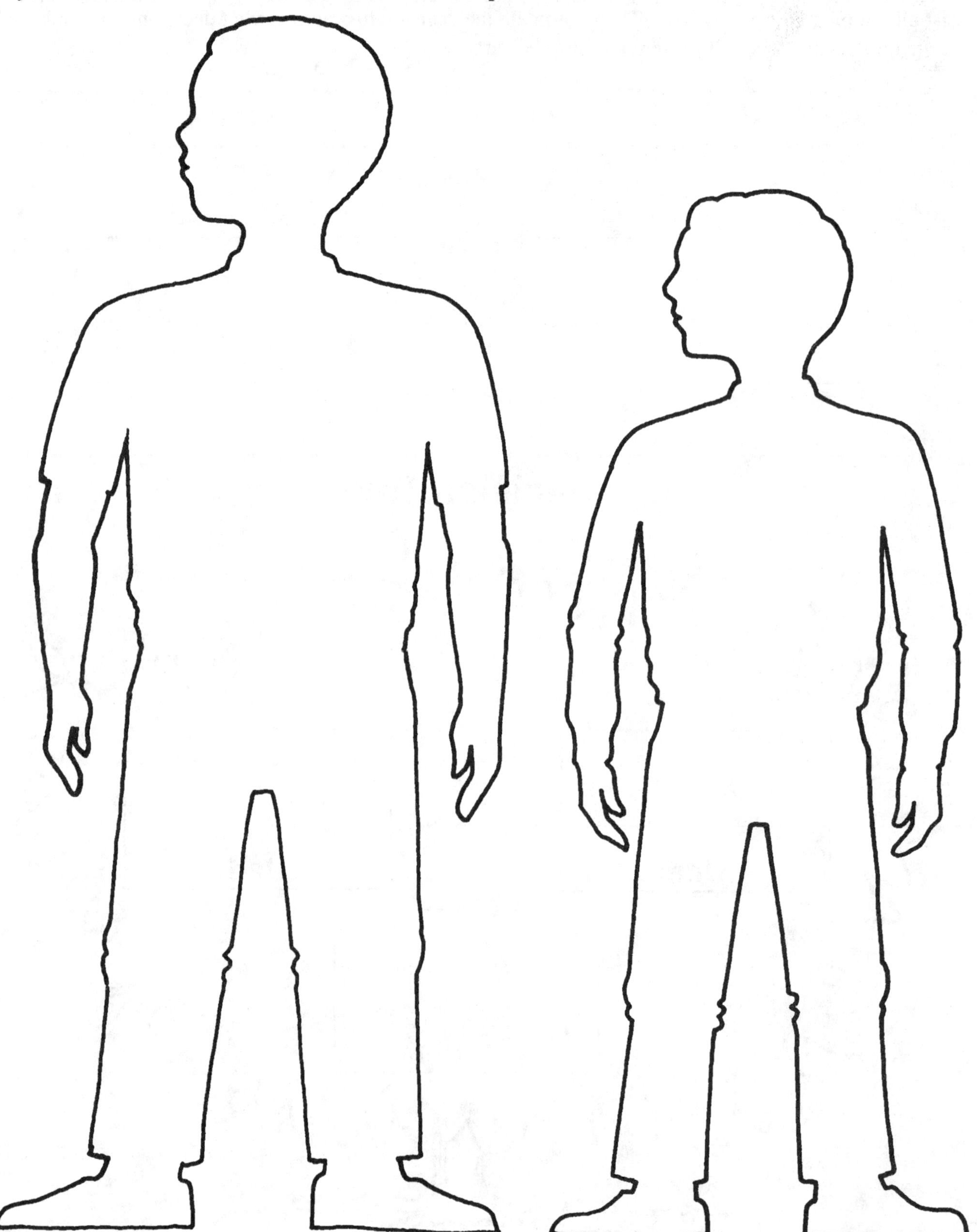

An Island Christmas

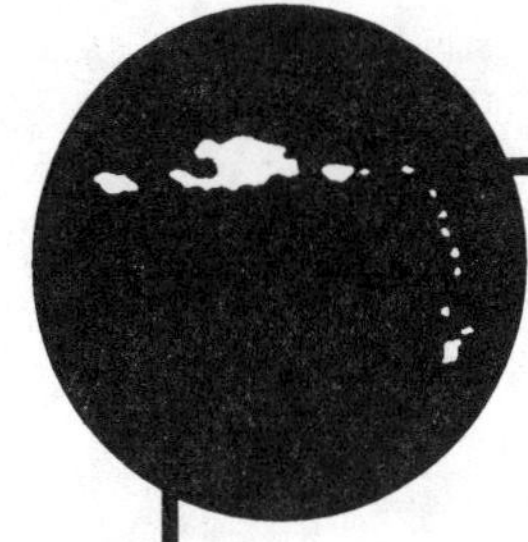

Author: Lynn Joseph

Illustrator: Catherine Stock

Publisher: Clarion, New York, 1992. 31 pages

Summary: A family celebrates the Christmas holiday in Trinidad and Tobago.

Background Information on Trinidad and Tobago:

Official Name: Republic of Trinidad and Tobago

Area: 5,130 square kilometers

Capital: Port of Spain

Population: 1,299,301 (1992)

Official Language: English

Major Religions: Roman Catholicism, Hinduism, Protestantism, Islam

Government: Republic

Monetary Unit: Dollar

Connecting Activities:

- Have students locate Trinidad and Tobago on the Caribbean map on page 43.

- Black currant cake is a popular holiday dish in Trinidad and Tobago. Have students make lists of their favorite Christmas or holiday foods.

- Some of the people in the parade play "shakers." Allow students to make shakers, using tin cans and beans.

- The young girl refers to the glide of a limbo dancer. The limbo can be fun. Using a broom handle, allow students to try the limbo. Challenge them to see who can go the lowest.

- The children decorate their tree with foil angels. Allow students to make angels out of aluminum foil.

- The Christmas holiday is rich in tradition for this family. Have students write about their favorite holiday traditions.

Caribbean Bibliography

Berry, James. *A Thief in the Village and Other Stories.* (Orchard Books, 1988)

Berry, James. *When I Dance.* (Harcourt, 1991)

Bryan, Ashley. *The Cat's Purr.* (Atheneum, 1985)

Bryan, Ashley. *Turtle Knows Your Name.* (Atheneum, 1989)

Dorris, Michael. *Morning Girl.* (Hyperion, 1992)

Greene, Carol. *Roberto Clemente: Baseball Superstar.* (Children's Press, 1991)

Greenfield, Eloise. *Under the Sunday Tree.* (Harper & Row, 1988)

Joseph, Lynn. *The Mermaid's Twin Sister: More Stories from Trinidad.* (Clarion, 1994)

Kincaid, Jamaica. *Annie John.* (Penguin, 1985)

Pomerantz, Charlotte. *The Chalk Doll.* (Lippincott, 1989)

Springer, Eintou Pearl. *The Caribbean: The Land and Its People.* (Silver Burdett, 1988)

Taylor, Theodore. *The Cay.* (Bantam, 1969)

Williams, Karen Lynn. *Tap-Tap.* (Clarion, 1994)

Map of the Caribbean

The Most Beautiful Place in the World

Author: Ann Cameron

Illustrator: Thomas B. Allen

Publisher: Knopf, New York, 1988. 57 pages

Summary: This story is about a motivated, energetic young boy who is abandoned by his mother and consequently lives with his grandmother. His dream is to go to school and learn to read.

Background Information on Guatemala:

Official Name: Republic of Guatemala

Area: 108,889 square kilometers

Capital: Guatemala City

Population: 9,784,275 (1992)

Official Language: Spanish

Major Religions: Roman Catholicism, Evangelical Christianity

Government: Republic

Monetary Unit: Quetzal

Connecting Activities:

- Have students locate Guatemala on the Central America map on page 47.

- Juan's mother abandons him when she falls in love with a man. She asks her mother to take care of Juan. Have students write the letter from Juan's mother to his grandmother explaining the situation and asking her to care for Juan.

- Juan usually eats warm tortillas for breakfast. Allow students to eat tortillas in class.

- Have students write a diary entry from Juan in which he explains how he feels about being left by his mother to live with his grandmother.

The Most Beautiful Place
in the World *(cont.)*

- Juan likes to go to San Juan at night and look at the lights. Allow students to make crayon resist night drawings by following the directions below.

Materials: crayons, including silver and white; black watercolor paint; white construction paper

<table>
<tr>
<td>

1. Draw a night scene, using mostly white and silver on the construction paper.

</td>
<td>

2. Lightly paint over the picture with black watercolor paint to simulate the night.

</td>
<td>

3. Allow pictures to dry, then hang them.

</td>
</tr>
</table>

- Juan's mother takes little or no interest in him. Have students discuss their opinions of Juan's mother.

- Ask students how they would define the word "smart." Then ask them whether they think Juan is smart according to their own definitions.

- Have students compare their own primary school experiences to what they think Juan's school experience is like.

- Juan's teachers wanted to promote him to second grade with his grandmother's permission. Have students write the letter from the teacher to the grandmother asking her for permission.

- Juan is worried that his grandmother might expect too much from him because she loves him so much. As a class discuss whether or not we tend to expect more from those we love.

- The story ends rather abruptly with no hint as to the futures of the characters. Have students predict the futures of the main characters.

- Juan feels that his town is the most beautiful place in the entire world. Ask students to consider what they think is the most beautiful place in the world. Then have them draw pictures and write about those special places.

Central America Bibliography

Aardema, Vera. *Borreguita and the Coyote.* (Knopf, 1991)

Anaya, Rudolfo A. *Bless Me, Ultima.* (Tonatiuh International, 1972)

Ashabranner, Brent. *Children of the Maya: A Guatemalan Indian Odyssey.* (Dodd, Mead, 1986)

Castaneda, Omar S. *Among the Volcanoes.* (Lodestar, 1991)

Delacre, Lulu. *Las Navidades: Popular Christmas Songs from Latin America.* (Scholastic, 1990)

Dorros, Arthur. *Abuela.* (Dutton, 1991)

Gray, Genevieve. *How Far, Felipe?* (Harper, 1978)

Hewett, Joan. *Laura Loves Horses.* (Clarion, 1990)

Lattimore, Deborah Nourse. *Why There Is No Arguing in Heaven.* (Waapoone Publishing, 1986)

Lewis, Richard. *All of You Was Singing.* (Atheneum, 1991)

Politi, Leo. *Three Stalks of Corn.* (Macmillan, 1976)

Roe, Eileen. *With My Brother.* (Bradbury, 1991)

Rohmer, Harriet. *The Legend of Food Mountain.* (Children's Book Press, 1982)

Rohmer, Harriet. *Uncle Nacho's Hat.* (Children's Book Press, 1989)

Rohmer, Harriet, Octavio Chow, & Morris Vidaure. *The Invisible Hunters.* (Children's Book Press, 1987)

Rohmer, Harriet & Dorminster Wilson. *Mother Scorpion Country.* (Children's Book Press, 1987)

Soto, Gary. *The Skirt.* (Delacorte, 1992)

St. George, Judith. *Panama Canal: Gateway to the World.* (Putnam, 1989)

Winter, Jeanette. *Diego.* (Knopf, 1991)

Map of Central America

Number the Stars

Author: Lois Lowry

Publisher: Houghton Mifflin, Boston, 1989. 132 pages

Summary: Annemarie and her family must protect their Jewish friends as the German soldiers take over Copenhagen, Denmark.

Background Information on Denmark:

Official Name: Kingdom of Denmark

Area: 43,069 square kilometers

Capital: Copenhagen

Population: 5,163,955 (1992)

Official Language: Danish

Major Religion: Evangelical Lutheranism

Government: Constitutional Monarchy

Monetary Unit: Danish Krone

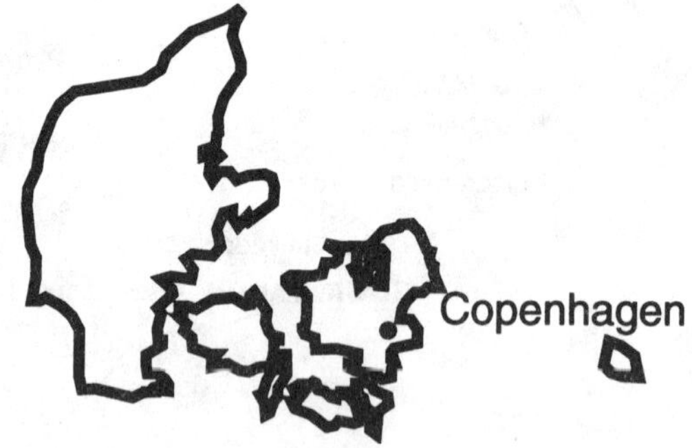

Connecting Activities:

(Chapters 1-4)

• Have students locate Denmark on the Europe map on page 61.

• Annemarie and Ellen practice running for the races they planned to participate in at school. Allow students to have races either at recess or during physical education period.

• The children in Denmark are all familiar with the fairy tales of Hans Christian Andersen because he is from Denmark. Have students choose their favorite Andersen fairy tale to read to a child in another grade level. Perhaps this can be arranged with a first or second grade teacher at your school.

• Using the Europe map located on page 61, have students locate all the countries that were occupied by German soldiers.

Number the Stars (cont.)

- Throughout the story, have students keep a dialectical journal of their responses. In a dialectical journal, students choose quotes from the story that are particularly meaningful or powerful to them. They write down their quotes on one side of the page; on the other half of the page they write their responses to their quotes. It may be helpful for you to ask students to note the pages of the book their quotes are on.

The dialectical journal is set up like this:

Book Quote	**Your Response**
1. Redheaded Peter, her sister's fiancé, had not married anyone in the years since Lise's death.	1. This quote made me feel sad. Peter must be very lonely.
2. "It is what friends do," Mama had said.	2. This quote made me think of things that I can do for my friends.

- Once the Germans take over there is an 8:00 p.m. curfew. Ask students why they think there is such a curfew. Then, ask them what their own curfew is and whether or not they think it is a fair time.

- Have students do personality profiles of Annemarie and Ellen. What do they know about them from the book? What can they infer about their personalities? Are either of them brave?

- Have students do research on Hitler and why he wanted to "relocate" the Jews. Then, have them write brief reports of what they learned during the course of their research.

- Ellen really has a flair for the dramatic, as probably some of your own students do. Have students turn any scene from the book into a readers' theater script. In readers' theater, there are no props or scenery and no memorization of lines. Students simply read the lines directly from the script. You can divide the class so that half of the students write the script and the other half performs.

- As a result of the German occupation, the people in Denmark are running out of food and supplies. Sugar, butter, and leather are nonexistent, for example. Ask students what items they would miss most from their lives.

- Kirsti loves stories about kings and queens. Have students write a story involving a king or queen that would be appropriate for Annemarie to tell Kirsti.

Number the Stars (cont.)

- Kirsti remembers seeing fireworks on one of her birthdays. Although it was really a battle, her parents prefer that she believe it was fireworks. Have students do a crayon resist of a fireworks scene by following the directions below.

Materials: fluorescent crayons, construction paper, dark blue watercolor paints

1. Using fluorescent crayons, have students draw explosive fireworks on a piece of construction paper.

2. Using dark blue watercolors, paint over the entire piece of construction paper.

3. The crayons will resist the paint when it dries, making the fireworks scene stand out.

(Chapters 5-9)

- Ellen wants to be an actress when she grows up, but her father wants her to be a teacher like himself. Ask students what they want to be as adults. Then, ask them whether their parents have put any pressure on them about their decisions.

- Annemarie's father proves to the soldiers that Ellen is their daughter by showing them a picture. After seeing the picture, the soldier tears it up. Ask students why they think the soldier would do such a thing.

- Have students predict what would have happened if the German soldiers had figured out that Ellen was not Annemarie's sister.

- Have students draw pictures of Henrik's house using the descriptions provided in the novel. They may also wish to use their imaginations to fill in some details.

- Have students discuss in small groups what they think bravery means. Then, have them write personal stories about situations in which they think they have displayed bravery.

- As a class, discuss whether it is easier to be brave when you do not know everything about the situation.

Number the Stars *(cont.)*

- Annemarie and Ellen collect dried flowers to decorate Uncle Henrik's house. Using these directions, students can make dried flowers.

Materials: fresh cut flowers, nails, string, scissors, and a warm, dry, dark place to hang flowers

1. Cut the flowers before they are in full bloom and remove leaves.

2. Group flowers together using string to tie stems together. Do not bunch too tightly because the air needs to circulate in order to dry the blossoms.

3. Hang flowers upside down suspended from a nail in a warm, dry, dark place for three to five weeks.

(Chapters 10-17)

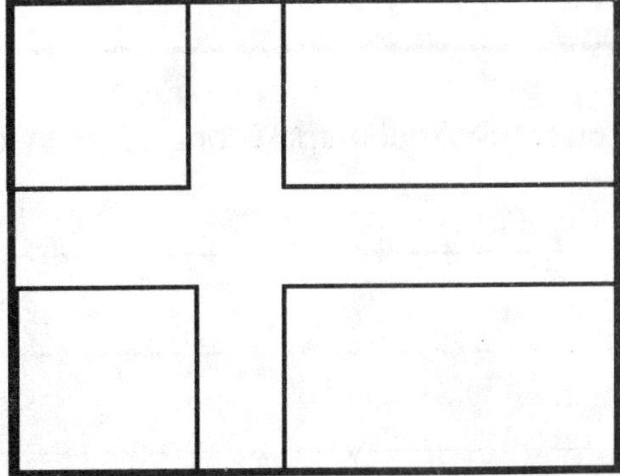

- Have students discuss why Annemarie's family does not try to go to Sweden under the circumstances.

- Have students write a good-bye letter to Annemarie from Ellen.

- Have students imagine that the Germans find out that Peter is with the resistance movement. Then, have them create a wanted poster for Peter.

- Have students make predictions for the following questions:

   What would have happened to Annemarie if the soldiers had figured out the plan regarding the handkerchief?

   What is the Rosen's life like in Sweden?

   Will the Rosens ever come back to live in Copenhagen?

- Peter wrote the Johansen family a final letter before he died. Have students draft what they think this letter may have said.

- Annemarie never considered herself to be a brave person. Have students detail her heroic actions, using the activity sheet on page 52.

- Have students research and draw the Danish flag.

Annemarie: Our Heroine

In spite of everything Annemarie did to help her friends, the Rosens, she still does not feel that she is brave. Using the chart below, chronicle all the brave, heroic actions Annemarie performs during the course of the story. Then, answer the question that follows on a separate piece of paper.

Annemarie's Bravery Chart

Chapters	Brave Actions
1-3	
4-6	
7-9	
10-12	
13-16	

Do you think Annemarie is brave? Why or why not?______________________________

____

____

____

The Gift

Author: Joan Lowery Nixon

Illustrator: Andrew Glass

Publisher: Macmillan, New York, 1983. 86 pages

Summary: Brian and his grandpa try to get the rest of the family to believe in the little people and leprechauns.

Background Information on Ireland:

Official Name: Republic of Ireland

Area: 70,284 square kilometers

Capital: Dublin

Population: 3,521,207 (1992)

Official Languages: Irish, English

Major Religion: Roman Catholicism

Government: Republic

Monetary Unit: Irish pound

Connecting Activities:

(Chapters 1-2)

- Have students locate Ireland on the Europe map on page 61.

- Ask students whether they believe in UFO's, ghosts, little people, or leprechauns.

- Brian and his grandpa believe that little people can cause a great deal of mischief. Have students write stories about little people causing mischief in their own houses.

- Brian suspects that the cat can tell what he is thinking. Have students discuss whether or not they believe that animals can think. Then ask them what they think animals think about.

The Gift *(cont.)*

- Brian's grandpa taught him that you can hear sounds better when you really concentrate. Have students make a class list of all the normal sounds of the classroom. Then, have them listen carefully for three minutes to all the sounds they may not have noticed before. Make a list of the new sounds. Then, compare the two lists.

- Brian is so happy to be with his grandpa. Have students express Brian's feelings of happiness through a picture, essay, or poem.

(Chapters 3-4)

- Ireland is very cold when Brian is visiting. Have students research the weather and seasons in Ireland.

- Brian sends his friend, Charlie, postcards from Ireland. Have students make a postcard, using the activity sheet on page 55, to send to his friend Charlie.

- Brian's grandpa and Aunt Nora tell him stories of their childhood. Have students ask relatives to tell stories from their childhoods for the students to share with the class.

- Nora is very angry that her father is telling Brian stories about little people and leprechauns. Have students write a conversation between Nora and her father in which she chastises him for telling Brian such "crazy" stories.

(Chapters 5-7)

- Have students discuss what they think Brian's parents would think about his grandfather telling him stories of little people and leprechauns.

- Have students predict what they think Nora says to Brian's parents when she speaks to them on the phone.

- Have students write what they think will happen in the last chapter of the story.

- Have students draw what Brian sees when he first finds the little people.

- Have students predict how they think Charlie will react when Brian tells him the story of the little people.

- Have students write an essay describing what they think "the gift" is.

Postcard to Charlie

Use this side of the postcard to record what Brian will write to Charlie from Ireland. Do not forget to make up an address for Charlie. Then, cut out the postcard and on the reverse side, draw a fancy picture of Ireland.

Grandfather's Rock

Author: Joel Strangis

Illustrator: Ruth Gamper

Publisher: Houghton Mifflin, Boston, 1993. 29 pages

Summary: A family struggles with the decision of what to do with their elderly grandfather.

Background Information on Italy:

Official Name: Italian Republic

Area: 301,287 square kilometers

Capital: Rome

Population: 57,904,628 (1992)

Official Language: Italian

Major Religion: Roman Catholicism

Government: Republic

Monetary Unit: Lira

Connecting Activities:

- Have students locate Italy on the Europe map on page 61.

- Have students write about the ways in which their own lives would change if a relative were to move in with their family.

- Grandfather tells stories about his adventures on the sea and of strange people and beautiful places. Have students write any one of these stories.

- Have students discuss in small groups what advice they would give the father about where the grandfather should live.

- Have students write a readers' theater script for the story. Then several students could volunteer to dramatize the story for the rest of the class.

- Have students write the conversation that may have existed between the mother and the father as he explains to her why he has brought grandfather back home.

I-Know-Not-What, I-Know-Not-Where

Adapted By: Eric Kimmel

Illustrator: Robert Sauber

Publisher: Holiday House, New York, 1994. 63 pages

Summary: A Russian tale about a man who will do anything to save the life of a beautiful white dove.

Background Information on Russia:

Official Name: Russian Federation

Area: 17,075,400 square kilometers

Capital: Moscow

Population: 149,527,479 (1992)

Official Language: Russian

Major Religion: Eastern Orthodox

Government: Republic

Monetary Unit: Ruble

Connecting Activities:

(Chapters 1-2)

• Have students locate Russia on the Europe map on page 61.

• Have students discuss how they think the father would have decided which son would serve the czar if Frol had not volunteered to do so himself.

• Frol was often praised by his officers for his bravery. Ask students to make a special award for the officers to give Frol in honor of his bravery.

• Frolya weaved a beautiful carpet for Frol to sell. Have students design what they think the carpet looked like by using colored chalk on a piece of construction paper. Use hair spray to seal the chalk design.

I-Know-Not-What, I-Know-Not-Where

(cont.)

- Frol's white dove, Frolya, tells him the most magnificent stories. Have students write any of the stories that are listed in the book. The examples include stories about: a princess with magic powers who was turned into a bird by an evil wizard's spell, a dead czar who lived in a fiery pit, a cat as big as a mountain, an old witch who lived in a small house and walked on chicken feet, and three enormous giants who lived beneath a glass mountain.

- Have students debate whether or not they think Frol should have given the dove to Bakbul.

- Ask students whether they think Bakbul will heed the warnings of the imps.

(Chapters 3-4)

- Ask students whether they think Bakbul should trust the advice of his wife.

- Frolya tells Frol that "morning is wiser than evening." Ask students to what extent they agree or disagree with this and to offer examples to support their opinions.

- Frolya tells Frol that while he is looking for the Land of Nine Times Nine he should not close his eyes. Challenge students to see how long they can keep their eyes open without blinking.

- Have students discuss why the dove does not just give herself to the czar to save Frol from all the trouble he is going through.

- Baba Yaga is a popular character in Russian tales. Challenge students to read another Russian folktale involving Baba Yaga. For suggestions see the Europe bibliography on page 60.

- Have students predict how the grandmother frog will help Frol.

(Chapters 5-6)

- Have students discuss what the frog may have meant by all the world is a narrow bridge and to never be afraid of anything.

I-Know-Not-What, I-Know-Not-Where

(cont.)

- The frog really enjoys hearing riddles and trying to solve them. Have students create or research riddles. Then have them make an "envelope" riddle book for the class by following the directions below.

Materials: envelopes, index cards, pens

1. Write the riddle on the front of an envelope.
2. Write the answer to the riddle on the index card.
3. Place the index card in the envelope.
4. Staple all the envelopes together to make a class riddle book.

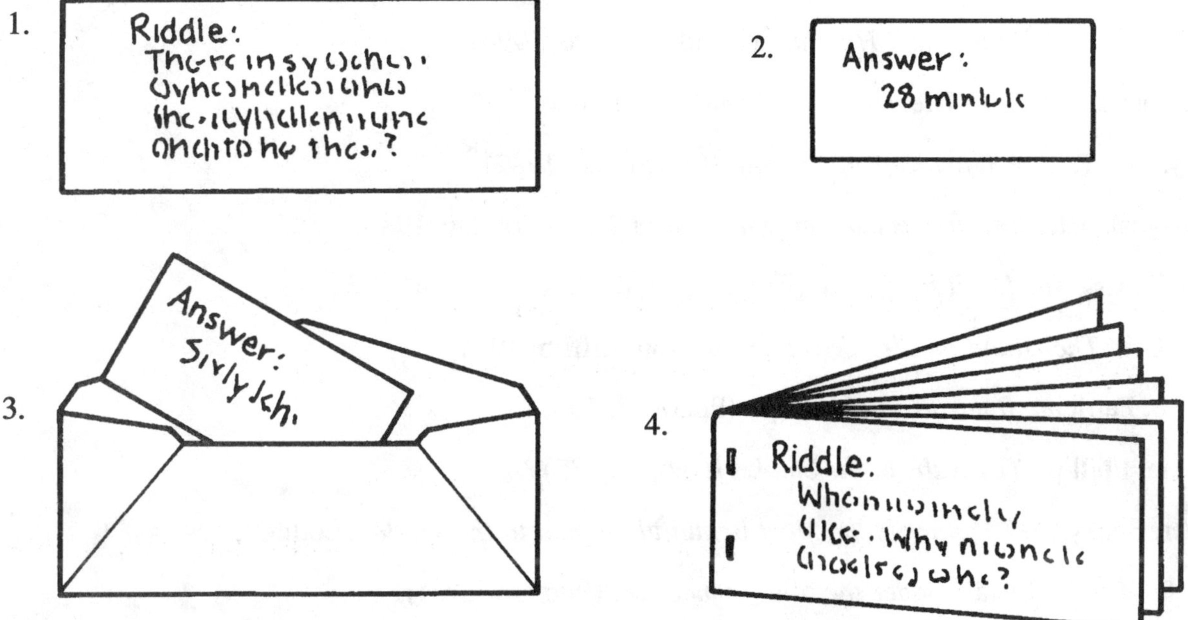

- Have students draw the flying ship Frol used to return to Frolya.

- Have students predict whether Frol will make it back to the czar.

(Chapters 7-8)

- Bakbul killed the white dove. Have students write up a punishment as if they were judges hearing about what Bakbul did to the dove.

- In small groups, students predict what will happen when the czar finds out that the white dove was reborn and turned into a beautiful woman who married Frol.

- This story is an old one told from one person to the next until it became well known. Discuss with students how stories change as they are passed from one person to the next and often become greatly exaggerated. You may even allow students to play a quick game of "telephone" wherein a message starts with one person and is passed on to several others. The last person to hear the message repeats it to the first person to see how much it has changed as it was passed on. After students understand this concept, have them rewrite the story as they think it was originally told.

Europe Bibliography

Allen, Judy. *Seal.* (Candlewick Press, 1993)

Banks, Lynne Reid. *Melusine.* (HarperCollins, 1988)

Barrie, Barbara. *Lone Star.* (Bantam, 1990)

Bawden, Nina. *The Real Plato Jones.* (Clarion, 1993)

Blake, Robert J. *Dog.* (Philomel, 1994)

Croll, Carolyn. *The Little Snowgirl: An Old Russian Tale.* (Putnam, 1989)

Denise, Christopher. *The Fool of the World and the Flying Ship.* (Philomel, 1994)

de Tagyos, Paul Ratz. *A Coney Tale.* (Clarion, 1992)

Grauer, Rita. *Vasalisa and Her Magic Doll.* (Philomel, 1994)

Greene, Ellin. *Billy Bag and His Bull.* (Holiday House, 1994)

Hollinshead, Marilyn. *The Nine Days Wonder.* (Philomel, 1994)

Kelley, Eric P. *The Trumpeter of Krakow.* (Macmillan, 1982)

Micolaycak, Charles. *Babushka: An Old Russian Tale.* (Holiday, 1984)

Orgel, Doris. *The Devil in Vienna.* (Penguin, 1978)

Orlev, Uri. *The Island on Bird Street.* (Houghton Mifflin, 1984)

Polacco, Patricia. *Bubushka Baba Yaga.* (Philomel, 1993)

Pullman, Phillip. *The Ruby in the Smoke.* (Knopf, 1985)

Reyher, Becky. *My Mother Is the Most Beautiful Woman in the World.* (Lothrop, 1945)

Schaefer, Carole Lexa. *Under the Midsummer Sky.* (Putnam, 1994)

Schotter, Roni. *That Extraordinary Pig of Paris.* (Philomel, 1994)

Wooding, Sharon. *The Painter's Cat.* (Putnam, 1994)

Map of Europe

The Three Princes

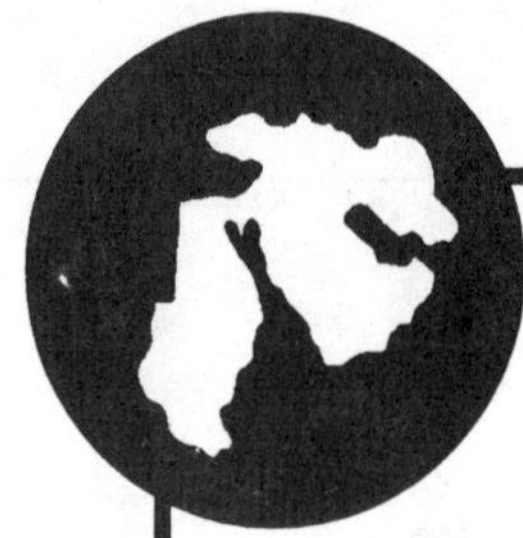

Retold By: Eric Kimmel

Illustrator: Leonard Everett Fisher

Publisher: Holiday House, New York, 1994. 26 pages

Summary: A Middle Eastern princess must choose among three princes to marry.

Background Information:

This story does not originate from a particular country. It is simply labeled as a Middle Eastern tale.

Connecting Activities:

- Ask students whom they think the princess should marry: Fahad, Muhammed, or Mohsen. Then have students write her letters expressing their views on whom she should give her hand to in marriage.

- One of the princes finds a magic carpet to give to the princess. Allow students to make a magical colored carpet by coloring a piece of white construction paper. Add glitter for sparkle.

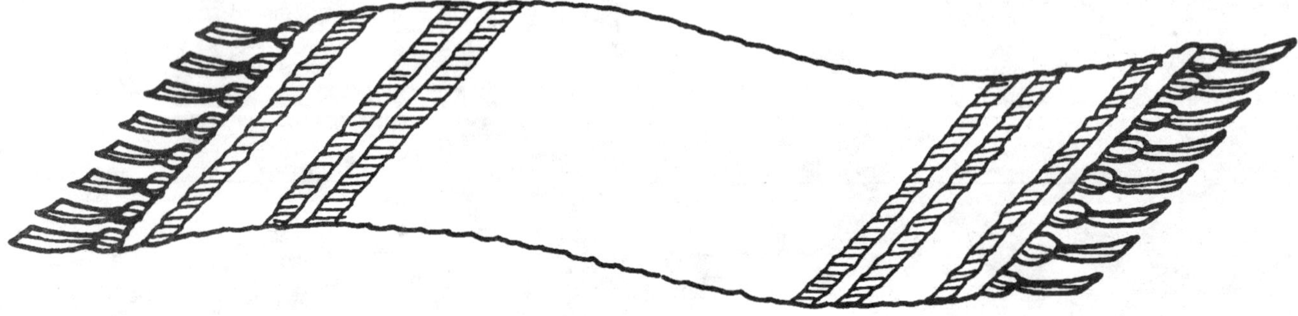

- The wedding of the princess and Mohsen is surely going to be an extravaganza in the village. Allow students to make special wedding invitations to the princess and Mohsen's wedding.

- The people of the village will no doubt want something special with which to remember the wedding day. Have students draw wedding pictures of the princess and Mohsen for all to enjoy.

- Now that the princess has chosen Mohsen, what will become of the other two princes? Have students write stories about the other two princes finding their brides.

- One of the reasons that the princess chose Mohsen was because without his crystal ball the princess would not have known that she was sick. Have students discuss what they think was wrong with the princess.

The Legend of the Persian Carpet

Author: Tomie dePaola

Illustrator: Claire Ewart

Publisher: Putnam, New York, 1993. 27 pages

Summary: When the King's diamond is stolen, the people of the village weave a carpet, hoping it will be as brilliant as the diamond.

Background Information On Iran:

Official Name: Islamic Republic of Iran

Area: 1,648,000 square kilometers

Capital: Tehran

Population: 61,183,138 (1992)

Official Language: Persian (Farsi)

Major Religions: Islam, Zoroastrianism, Christianity

Government: Theocratic Republic

Monetary Unit: Rial

Connecting Activities:

- Have students locate Iran on the Middle East map on page 74.

- Have students draw the palace.

- The thief not only steals the diamond, but because of his carelessness it falls and shatters. Have students determine a proper punishment for him.

- The thief must be captured and punished for his crime. Use the activity sheet located on page 64 to create a "wanted" poster.

- Have students write a diary entry for the king to describe how he felt the day the diamond was stolen.

- The king dreads telling his people about the diamond being stolen. Have students write a speech for the king to give to his people.

- Have students draw the special carpet the people made for the king. They can add silver glitter for sparkle.

Create a Poster

Create a wanted poster for the thief who stole the diamond from the king.

Wanted!

Description:

Crime:

Reward:

Becoming Gershona

Author: Nava Semel/ Translated by Seymour Simckes

Publisher: Penguin, New York, 1990. 150 pages

Summary: Gershona is not very popular among the neighborhood children. However, after her grandfather returns to Israel, and after she meets a new boy in the neighborhood, Gershona learns how to be a good friend and get along with others.

Background Information on Israel:

Official Name: State of Israel

Area: 20,770 square kilometers

Capital: Jerusalem

Population: 5,200,000 (1992)

Official Languages: Hebrew, Arabic

Major Religions: Judaism, Islam, Christianity

Government: Parliamentary Democracy

Monetary Unit: New Shekel

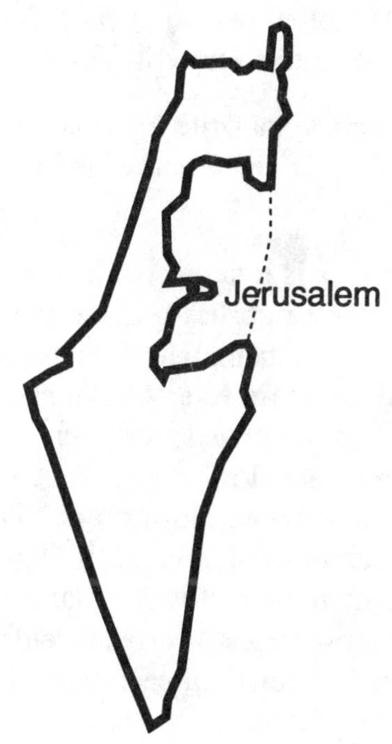

Connecting Activities:

(Chapters 1-5)

- Have students locate Israel on the Middle East map on page 74.

- Discuss what would make Gershona's father buy a car when he does not even know how to drive.

- Gershona is not very popular and really has no friends. Have students complete the brainstorm activity sheet, page 69, which asks them to consider what makes a good friend. Then have them write a letter to Gershona offering her advice on friendship.

- Gershona is very excited to have some time alone in her family's apartment. Ask students to brainstorm what they think Gershona is hoping to find when she is "snooping" around. Then ask them what they like to do when they have their houses to themselves.

Becoming Gershona (cont.)

- Simha moved to Israel from Libya. Have students locate Libya on the Middle East map on page 74.

- Gershona has several nicknames. Some of the neighborhood kids call her Gershona Primadonna. Her father sometimes calls her Gershonita. Ask students whether they have had nicknames that they either liked or disliked. Then ask them what nickname they might like to have.

- Simha always offers Gershona cocoa to drink. Allow students to have cocoa one morning.

- Sometimes Gershona spends time with Hemda and Avigdor even though they do not like her and do not treat her very well. One day when Gershona is spending time with them, their cousin Haggai is visiting from his kibbutz. Challenge students to find out what a kibbutz is.

- Have students write a position statement to respond to Avigdor's comment that "cars are for men."

- Gershona wondered whether or not a blind person can cry. Ask students what they think. Then, invite a blind person to your class to discuss his/her experiences with the students. Prepare students by asking them to write down questions prior to the visit.

- Have students write a prequel to the story in which the story is told about what happened between Gershona's grandmother and grandfather which caused him to leave Israel and eventually ask her for a divorce.

- Gershona is infatuated with plants. She plants radishes because she likes to eat them. Her friends plant all kinds of flowers. Gershona becomes frustrated when her radishes are slow to sprout. Allow students to plant flowers or vegetables of their choice. Then, have them predict which plants will grow fastest. Have students chart the growth of each type of plant to determine the rate of growth for each type using the activity sheet on page 70.

- Have students write letters Gershona's grandfather might have sent to her grandmother asking her for a divorce.

(Chapters 6-10)

- Gershona grows flowers and collects colored napkins in her spare time. Make a class chart of favorite free time activities among your students.

Becoming Gershona *(cont.)*

- In small groups students can discuss and predict how they think Gershona's relationship with her grandfather will progress.

- Gershona is named after her mother's brother Gershon. Ask students to find out how their parents decided on their names. What other names were proposed? Then, ask students what names they might prefer to have.

- Gershona often feels that she has no one to talk to. She has many questions about her culture and about growing up. Have students imagine that they are Gershona. Have them write letters to an advice columnist asking for advice.

- When Gershona is snooping in the apartment she finds a picture of a man in a uniform hidden under her mother's nightgown. Have students predict who they think the man in the photo is.

- As a class, have students discuss why the sprouting of Gershona's plants is so important to her. Then have them write about something that is very important to them.

- Gershona reads the stock pages to her grandfather each day. Bring in a newspaper and teach students how to read the stock pages.

- Gershona has a very different relationship with each of the characters in the story. Have students complete the relationship chart on page 71.

(Chapters 11–15)

- Gershona's teacher taught a lesson on flowers of Israel. Have students research to find out popular flowers in their home state, as well as the state flower for all other states. They can use the activity sheet on page 72 to record their answers.

- When Gershona sees that her friend's garden is growing very well, she becomes angry. To deal with her anger she tramples all of her friends flowers. Have students discuss in small groups how Gershona could have better dealt with her anger and frustration. Then, have them choose the best group solution to share with the rest of the class.

- Have students predict what happened to Nimrod's mother.

Becoming Gershona (cont.)

- Gershona comes to really enjoy the walks she takes with her grandfather. Ask students to take a walk with a grandparent, or other relative, or special friend. Then, ask them to write about the experience.

- When Gershona's father went to get his father, he had to wear a sign with his name on it so his father would know who he was. Have students write the first conversation that may have taken place between Gershona's father and his own father upon this initial meeting.

- As a class students can discuss the reasons Nimrod may have left without saying good-bye to Gershona. Then, have them write letters from either Nimrod to Gershona explaining why he left, or from Gershona to Nimrod describing how she felt when he left without saying good-bye to her.

- When Gershona and her father have a heart-to-heart talk, he tells her he is surprised at how much she has grown up. He tells her that soon she will have her bat mitzvah. Have students research what a bat mitzvah is and write a simple report to document what they have learned.

(Chapters 16-20)

- Have students discuss whether or not they think Gershona would like to have a sibling. Then have them discuss how her life will change with a new baby in the house.

- In small groups, have students discuss why Avigdor likes Gershona now after being so mean to her in the past.

- Gershona and her grandfather share a special moment when they free the fish into the Yarkon River. Ask students to draw a picture of this occasion.

- Simha does not believe children can have worries. Have students write essays to respond to Simha's belief.

- Nimrod shared a favorite legend about bulrushes with Gershona. Have students read a legend and then share the story with the class.

- Have students predict whether or not they think Avigdor and Gershona will get together now that Nimrod is out of the picture.

- Have students read "About this Book" on pages 152 and 153 of *Becoming Gershona.*

What Is a Friend?

Gershona does not have any real friends until she meets Nimrod. Perhaps she does not know how to make friends or how to be a good friend. Use the brainstorm chart below to record the ways you make friends and what qualities you think make a good friend. Use this information to write a letter to Gershona offering her advice on friendship.

What qualities make a good friend?	How do you make friends

Growth Chart

Use this chart to record the growth of the flower or vegetable you selected to plant.

	⅛"	¼"	½"	¾"	1"	1¼"	1½"	1¾"	2"
Day 14									
Day 13									
Day 12									
Day 11									
Day 10									
Day 9									
Day 8									
Day 7									
Day 6									
Day 5									
Day 4									
Day 3									
Day 2									
Day 1									

Describing Gershona

Use this chart to record Gershona's relationship with the following characters from the story: her mother, father, grandmother, grandfather, Nimrod, Simha, Hemda, and Avigdor.

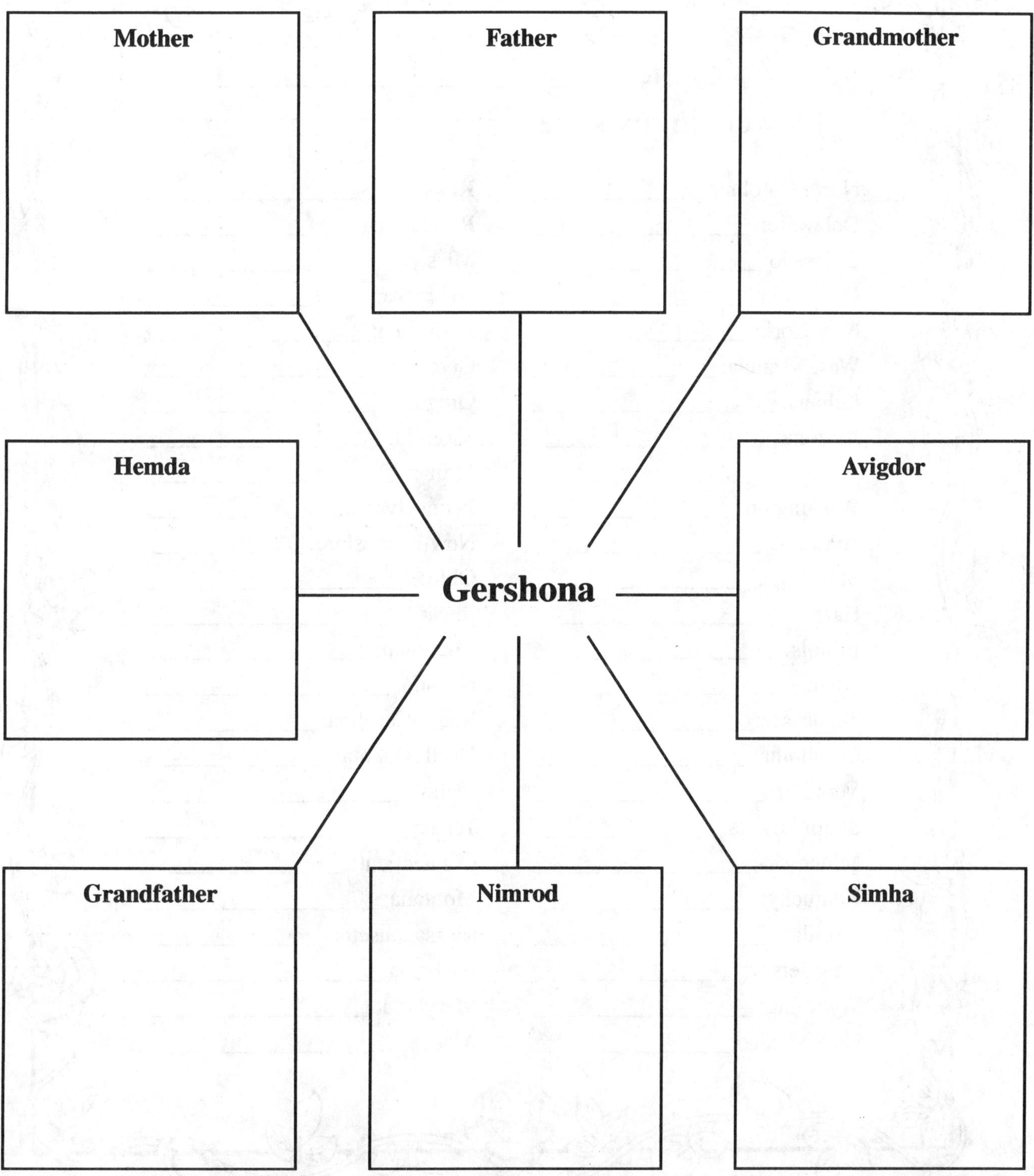

State Flowers

List the common flowers in your own state, then research the state flower for the rest of the states in the country.

My State_______________________________

Flowers in my state: _____________________

North Carolina: ____________	Kansas: ________________
Delaware: ______________	Rhode Island: ____________
Colorado:______________	Missouri:______________
California: ______________	Nebraska: ______________
New York: ______________	Louisiana: ______________
West Virginia: ___________	Georgia:______________
Indiana: ______________	Oregon: ______________
Arizona:______________	Virginia: ______________
Wisconsin:______________	Maine: ______________
Washington: ___________	Pennsylvania: ___________
Arkansas:______________	New Hampshire: __________
Mississippi:___________	Ohio: ______________
Hawaii: ______________	Iowa: ______________
Illinois: ______________	Michigan: ____________
Utah: ______________	Nevada: ______________
Tennessee:____________	South Carolina: __________
Oklahoma:____________	North Dakota: ____________
Vermont: ____________	Idaho: ______________
South Dakota: _________	Texas: ______________
Minnesota:____________	Connecticut: ___________
Kentucky: ____________	Montana: ______________
Florida: ______________	Massachusetts: __________
New Jersey:___________	Alabama:______________
Wyoming: ____________	Maryland: ____________
New Mexico:__________	Alaska: ______________

Middle East Bibliography

Haskins, Jim. *Count Your Way Through the Arab World.* (Carolrhoda Books, 1991)

Heide, Florence Parry & Judith Heide. *The Day of Ahmed's Secret.* (Lothrop, Lee & Shepard, 1990)

Heide, Florence Parry & Judith Heide. *Sami and the Time of Troubles.* (Clarion, 1992)

Orlev, Uri. *Lydia, Queen of Palestine.* (Houghton Mifflin, 1993)

Sadiq, Nazneen. *Camels Can Make You Homesick and Other Stories.* (Lorimer & Company, 1985)

Schami, Rafik. *A Hand Full of Stars.* (Dutton, 1990)

Staples, Suzanne Fisher. *Shabanu: Daughter of the Wind.* (Knopf, 1989)

Travers, P.L. *Two Pairs of Shoes.* (Viking, 1980)

Weston, Mark. *The Land and People of Pakistan.* (HarperCollins, 1992)

Map of the Middle East

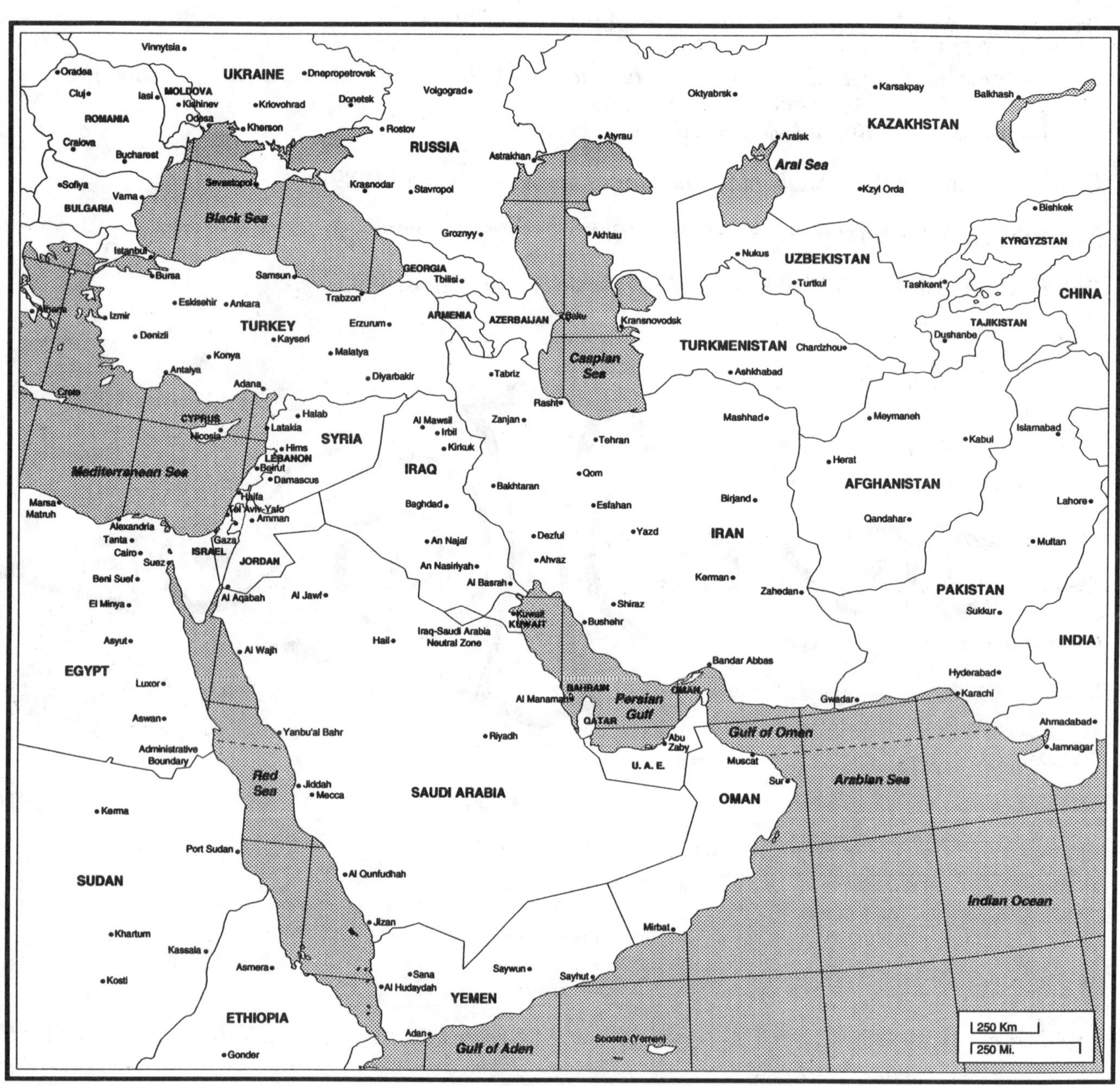

Anne of Green Gables

Author: L.M. Montgomery

Publisher: Watermill Press, 1985. 350 pages

Summary: An orphan finds a home with two unlikely people and lives the life about which she has always dreamed.

Background Information on Canada:

Official Name: Canada

Area: 9,922,330 square kilometers

Capital: Ottawa

Population: 25,354,064 (1986)

Official Language: French and English

Major Religions: Roman Catholic, Protestant

Government: Federal Union

Monetary Unit: Canadian dollar

Connecting Activities:

Chapter 1-5

- Rachel Lynde is known as the town gossip. Have students write a gossip column from Mrs. Lynde's point of view based on the people of Green Gables.

- Using the author's rich descriptions, ask students to draw a picture of Anne.

- Challenge students to find Prince Edward Island on a map.

- Anne likes to rename the places she encounters in her community. Have students choose five of their favorite places in their community. They should give each place new names that really suit that place.

- Have students predict what Marilla would have done if she were the one who went to pick up the orphan at the station and found a girl instead of a boy. Would she have taken Anne home as Matthew did?

- Have students predict what the conversation would have been if Matthew had driven Anne to Mrs. Spencer's home.

Anne of Green Gables (cont.)

Chapters 6-9

- In small groups have students discuss why Matthew likes Anne so much.

- Have students predict how Anne's life would be different if her parent had lived. What would she be like?

- Ask students if they think Marilla secretly wants Anne to stay.

- Have students imagine that they are a bug on the wall when Marilla tells Anne that she can stay at Green Gables. Then, have them write a descriptive essay describing what Anne's reaction was to the exciting news.

- Green Gables is rich with beautiful flowers and trees. Have students research any flower mentioned in the story and write a brief report to share with the rest of the class.

- Challenge students to keep a dictionary of new words as they read the story. (There are many new Canadian terms in the book).

- Ask students what they think would be appropriate punishment for Anne's reaction to Mrs. Lynde's comments.

- Anne gave a very dramatic apology to Mrs. Lynde. Ask for student volunteers to reenact this melodramatic monologue.

Chapters 10-15

- Anne describes her dream dress in detail. Have students draw this dress.

- Ask students to use a Venn diagram to compare and contrast Anne and Marilla's personalities.

- The circumstances surrounding the disappearance of Marilla's brooch are confusing. Have students write a diary entry from Anne's point of view describing the day, the situation, and her feelings.

- Anne would rather be pretty than smart. This is quite a quandary. As a class, discuss which is better, to be pretty or smart.

- Ask students to predict whether or not they think Anne will ever get married. What will her husband be like? What will she do with her life?

Chapters 16-22

- Canada has a different type of government system than the United States. Have students research to find out more about the Canadian government, then compare Canada's government to the United States' government.

- Explain to students that women did not always have the right to vote. Ask them to find out when women received the right to vote in the United States and Canada.

- Anne always says that she is a kindred spirit. Ask students what a kindred spirit is. Then ask if they consider themselves kindred spirits, or if anyone they know is a kindred spirit and why.

- Ask students why they think Marilla will not tell Anne how she really feels about her.

Anne of Green Gables *(cont.)*

Chapters 23-29

- Have students write an essay based on their opinion of the last sentence in chapter 24.

- Anne's school held a fund raiser to buy a flag for the school. Challenge your class to hold a fund raiser to purchase something that your school needs.

- Have students draw a picture of Anne before her hair disaster and after.

- Ask students to respond to this quote in chapter 28: "The things you wanted so much when you were a child don't seem half so wonderful to you when you get them."

- Have students write a conversation between Matthew and Marilla discussing their feelings about Anne's absence.

Chapters 30-38

- Ask students why Marilla would chastise Anne for reading novels.

- As a class discuss how life choices are different now for both men and women.

- Have students imagine that they are reporters and ask them to write an article for the local paper announcing Anne's achievement as number one in her class.

- Ask students to design a special diploma for Anne. They can use the bordered activity sheet on page 78.

- Anne has many ambitions. Ask students to list their ambitions along with a rationale for each. Encourage them to think of humanitarian ambitions as well as financial ones.

- Have students write a eulogy for Matthew. Then, ask for volunteers to read their eulogies as if they are Anne.

- After Matthew died Anne decided to turn down her scholarship and stay home with Marilla. Ask students what they would have done if they were in Anne's position.

- Have students predict what will happen in the future with Anne and Gilbert.

Anne's Diploma

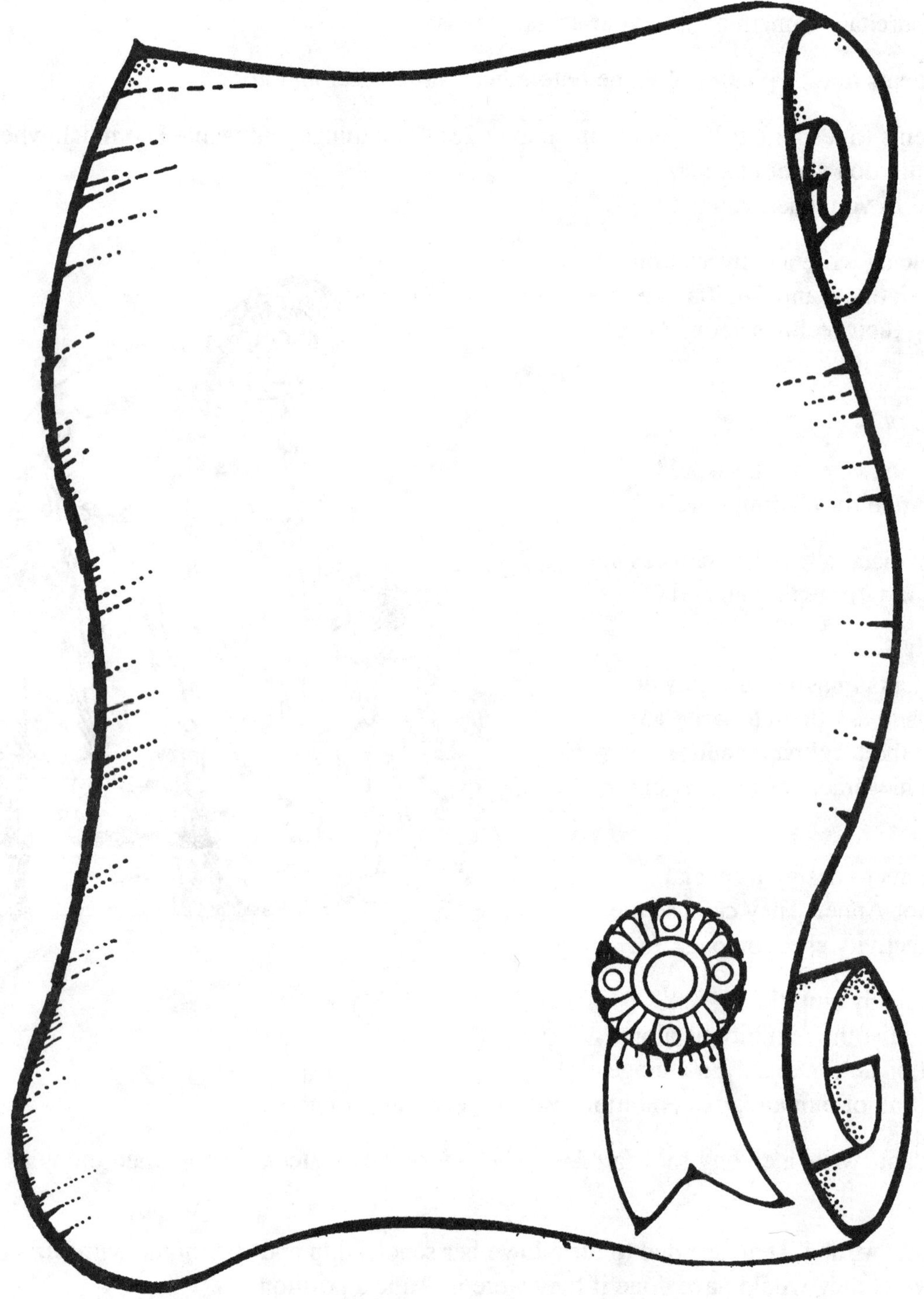

The Black Pearl

Author: Scott O'Dell

Publisher: Houghton Mifflin, Boston, 1967. 96 pages

Summary: Ramon wants to find a great black pearl; however, when he finds a great pearl, he is in for more trouble than he ever could have anticipated.

Background Information on Mexico:

Official Name: United Mexican States

Area: 1,958,201 square kilometers

Capital: Mexico City

Population: 92,380,721 (1992)

Official Language: Spanish

Major Religion: Roman Catholicism

Government: Republic

Monetary Unit: Peso

Connecting Activities:

(Chapters 1-3)

- Have students locate Mexico on the North America map on page 124.

- Challenge students to research the process of diving for pearls and how they are procured.

- The book describes in great detail what the Manta Diablo looks like. Have students draw a picture of the Manta Diablo, using the book's descriptions.

- In small groups have students discuss what they think the 'pearl of heaven' is.

- Ramon said his mother used to tell him stories about the Manta Diablo when he was a child to scare him into behaving. Have students write stories that their parents told them as children that were designed to teach them lessons.

The Black Pearl *(cont.)*

- Ramon is desperate to learn to dive; yet, his father will not take him diving. Have students discuss why Ramon's father does not want to take him sailing with the fleet.

- Ramon's responsibilities greatly differ from the type of responsibility a sixteen-year-old in the United States might have. Have students make a list of Ramon's responsibilities and what they believe to be a typical sixteen year old's responsibilities. Then, as a class discuss the differences of these two lists.

- Sevillano is able to hold his breath for four minutes. Using a timer, challenge students to see how long they can hold their breath. Then, have them compare their time to Sevillano's.

- The Manta Diablo is said to be ten feet wide. Have students measure how long this is.

- The divers that work for Ramon's father use a sink stone, a knife, and a rope. Today, scuba divers use a great deal of equipment when they go diving. Challenge students to make a list of all the equipment scuba divers use and the purpose of each piece of equipment.

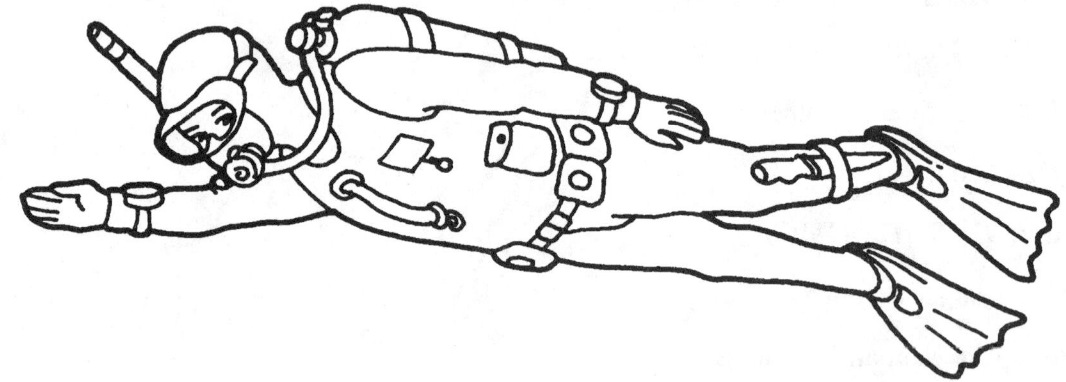

- The book describes in detail what Sevillano looks like. Challenge students to use the descriptions in the book to draw this character.

- Sevillano tells stories of great bravery and strength. However, most are greatly exaggerated. Have students write stories for Sevillano to tell the other divers.

- Although Ramon and Sevillano may appear to be very different people, they do have some similarities. Have students use the Venn diagram on page 83 to compare and contrast these two characters.

(Chapters 4–9)

- Have students respond to the following quote: "Be careful what you wish for because it just may come true."

- Although Ramon knows the serious risks of diving, he still wants to learn. Ask students whether, knowing all the risks involved, they would like to learn to dive.

- Ramon decides to take diving lessons without his father's permission. Have students role-play the conversation that may take place between Ramon and his father when he finds out Ramon is taking diving lessons without permission.

The Black Pearl (cont.)

- Have students write a paragraph expressing what they think of Luzon.

- Ramon's finding of the great pearl is big news. Have students write a news report announcing the big event. They can use the special newspaper on page 84 for this activity.

- Sevillano considers himself the greatest diver in the world. Have students predict how Sevillano will react when he finds out that Ramon has found the great black pearl.

- Mr. Salazar is trying to negotiate with the pearl dealers, but it is not going well. Have students imagine that they could give Mr. Salazar advice. For what price would they tell him to settle?

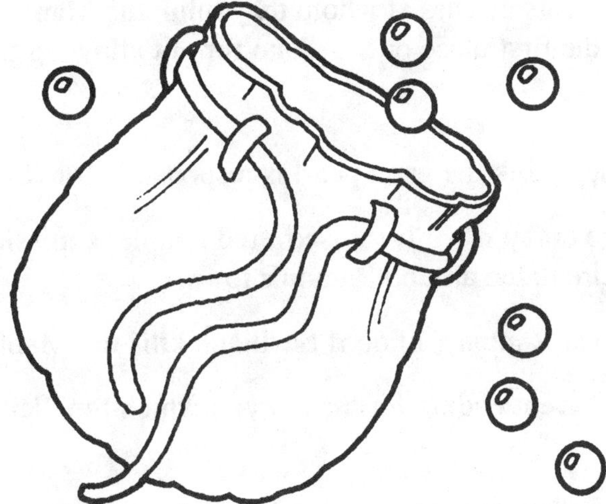

- When Mr. Salazar becomes frustrated with the pearl dealers, he decides to give the pearl to the church rather than sell it. Have students discuss why they think Mr. Salazar decided to do this.

- Have students compute the different offers made by the pearl dealers in American dollars. They can use the information on exchange rates from the local newspaper.

(Chapters 10-14)

- Ask students whether they think Ramon agreed with his father's decision to donate the pearl to the church.

- As a tribute to the Salazar family and the pearl, there is a big celebration in which the pearl is paraded around the town. Have students write a diary entry for Ramon for the day, describing what it was like to be such a celebrity.

- Sevillano is portrayed as an evil character throughout the book. Luzon believes in superstitions. Ask students whether they think either of these characters could have had anything to do with Ramon's father's fleet being lost at sea.

- There will be many drastic consequences to Ramon's father's death and the fleet being lost. Have students predict how the characters will be affected by his death and how it will affect the different aspects of their lives.

The Black Pearl (cont.)

- Now that his father has died, Ramon is beginning to wonder whether Luzon had been right. Have students write a letter from Ramon to Luzon expressing how they think Ramon feels now.

- Ramon decides to steal the pearl from the church. Have students predict what he is going to do with the pearl.

- Sevillano insists that Ramon go with him to try to sell the pearl. Have students predict what Sevillano will do with Ramon after the pearl is sold.

- Have students write an essay to describe what they think Sevillano meant when he said: "You toss it to the devil, and the devil picks it up."

- In small groups have students discuss at whom they think the Manta Diablo is most mad— Ramon for stealing the pearl in the first place or Sevillano for not allowing the pearl to be returned.

(Chapters 15-18)

- Ask students whether they think the great pearl is responsible for Ramon's father's death.

- Ramon's mother must go crazy when it is discovered that he is missing. Have students create a "missing" poster to be circulated around Ramon's town.

- Have students predict what Ramon will do if Sevillano kills the Manta Diablo.

- Have students write a different ending for the story in which Sevillano is not killed by the Manta Diablo.

- Have students discuss whether or not they think Sevillano gets what he deserves.

- Most of this story takes place in the ocean. Allow students to do a crayon resist ocean scene by following the directions below.

   Materials: brightly colored crayons, blue watercolors, and a paintbrush

   1. Using the crayons, draw an ocean scene. For best effect, press hard when coloring.

   2. Lightly paint over the drawing with blue watercolor paints.

   3. Allow to dry overnight.

Character Venn Diagram

Although Ramon and Sevillano may appear to be very different people, they are similar in some ways.
Use the Venn diagram below to record the ways in which Sevillano and Ramon are alike and the ways
in which they are different. In the outer portion of the diagram, record the ways in which the characters
are different. In the center portion where the circles join, record the ways in which the characters are
alike.

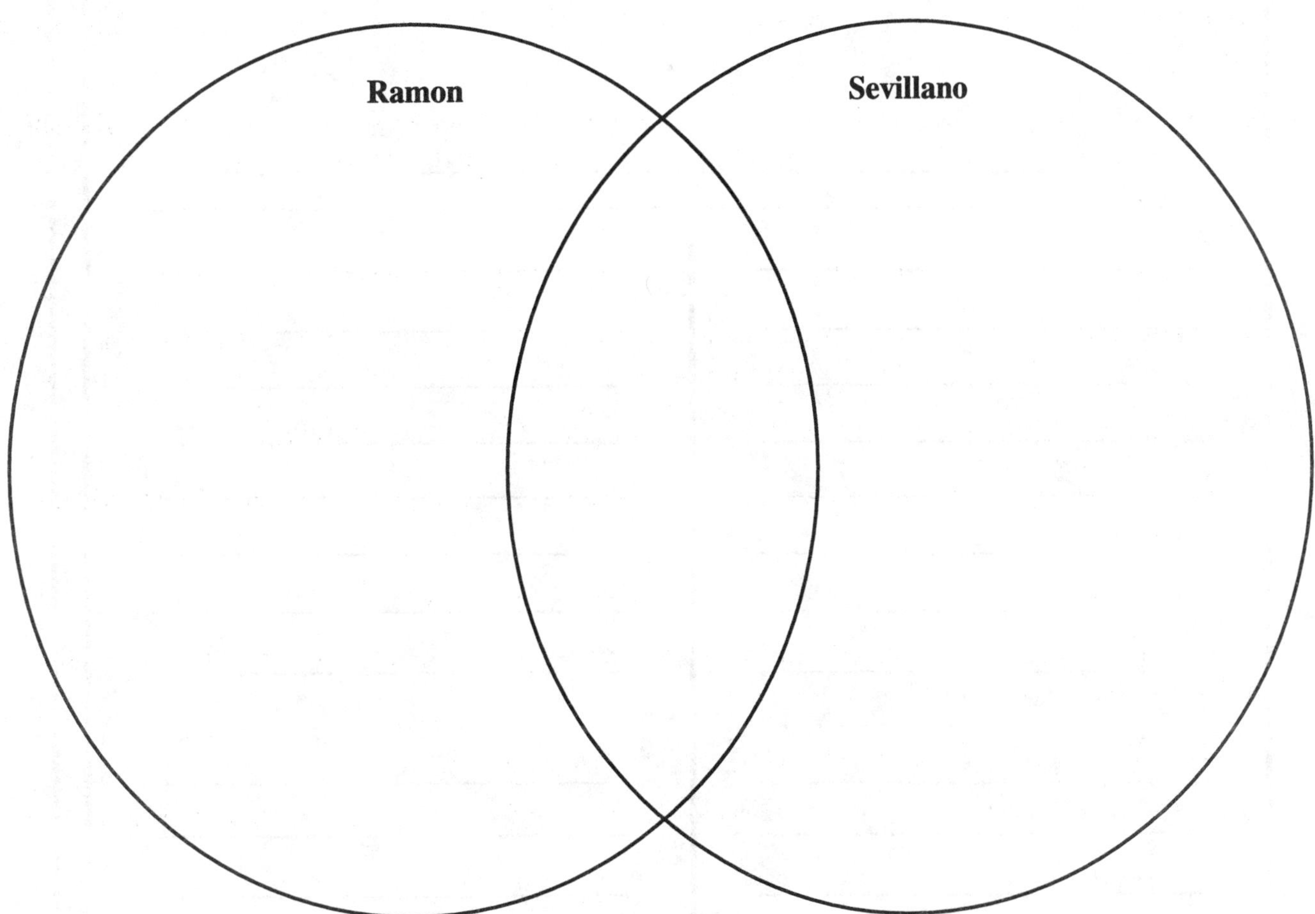

Extra! Extra!

When Ramon finds the great black pearl, it is big news in his community. Imagine that you are a newspaper journalist. Write a front page story about Ramon finding the pearl. Use your imagination to include community reaction and quotes from Ramon.

The Friendship and *The Gold Cadillac*

Author: Mildred D. Taylor

Illustrator: Michael Hays

Publisher: Bantam, New York, 1987. 87 pages

Summary: These two powerful short stories depict lives of African-Americans living during times of racial unrest.

Background Information on United States:

Official Name: United States of America

Area: 3,618,770 sq. mi. (9,372,571 square kilometers)

Capital: Washington, D.C.

Population: 256,300,000

Official Language: English

Major Religions: Protestant, Roman Catholic, Judaism, Mormonism, Eastern Orthodox, Islam, Buddhism

Government: Republic

Monetary Unit: Dollar

Connecting Activities:

"The Friendship"

- Cassie really enjoys looking through the 1933 catalog she found at the Wallace's store. Have students make a list of some of the items they think they would find in a 1933 catalog. Then have them draw a page of items from that catalog.

- Cassie often talks about the hot "Mississippi summer." Have students find out what the weather is like year-round in Mississippi.

- Dewberry is very disrespectful to Mr. Tom Bee just because he is black. Dewberry did not even care that Mr. Tom Bee is old enough to be his grandfather. Have students discuss how they feel about Dewberry's actions.

- Stacey always nervously reminds his brothers and sister to behave and keep quiet around the Wallace family. Ask students why they think Stacey does this.

The Friendship and
The Gold Cadillac *(cont.)*

- Have students predict how Tom Bee saved John Wallace many years ago.

- Cassie and her brothers love to hear Mr. Tom Bee's stories. Have students ask grandparents or other elders to tell favorite stories. Then have students write down the stories and collect them in a class book of popular old stories.

- John Wallace warns Tom Bee that if he does not show some respect, John will have to take some kind of action. Have students discuss in small groups why Tom Bee chooses to risk his life rather than call John "Mr. Wallace."

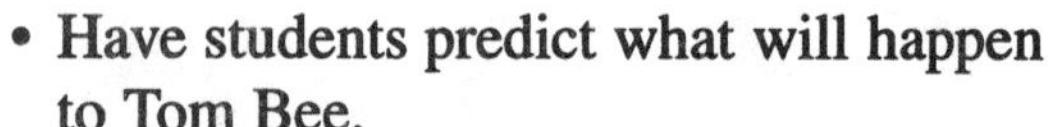

- Have students predict what will happen to Tom Bee.

- Ask students why they think Mildred Taylor decided to call this short story "The Friendship." Then ask students to write essays about what friendship means to them. Have them use the brainstorm activity sheet on page 87 prior to writing their essays.

- The story ends immediately following the shooting of Tom Bee so we do not know what the characters' reactions are to the event. Have students complete the reaction chart on page 88, describing how they think the characters reacted.

"The Gold Cadillac"

- Have students make a picture of the Cadillac. Allow them to use gold glitter to add sparkle to the picture.

- Ask students why they think Lois' father bought such a fancy car.

- Lois tells her mother that she does not like the way her mother is acting in regard to her father's purchase of the car. Have students discuss in small groups whether or not they think children should feel free to judge their parents' actions.

- Ask students why they think Lois' father sold the car after her mother agreed to let him keep it.

- Have students write an essay describing a time when they were treated as if they did not belong. Then ask them to try to make connections between that experience and what Lois' family is going through in the story.

- Have students research the civil rights movement.

Friendship

Mildred Taylor named her first short story "The Friendship." Consider what friendship means to you by completing the brainstorm web below. Then, answer the question that follows. After you have completed this prewriting exercise, you may begin writing your essay on what friendship means to you.

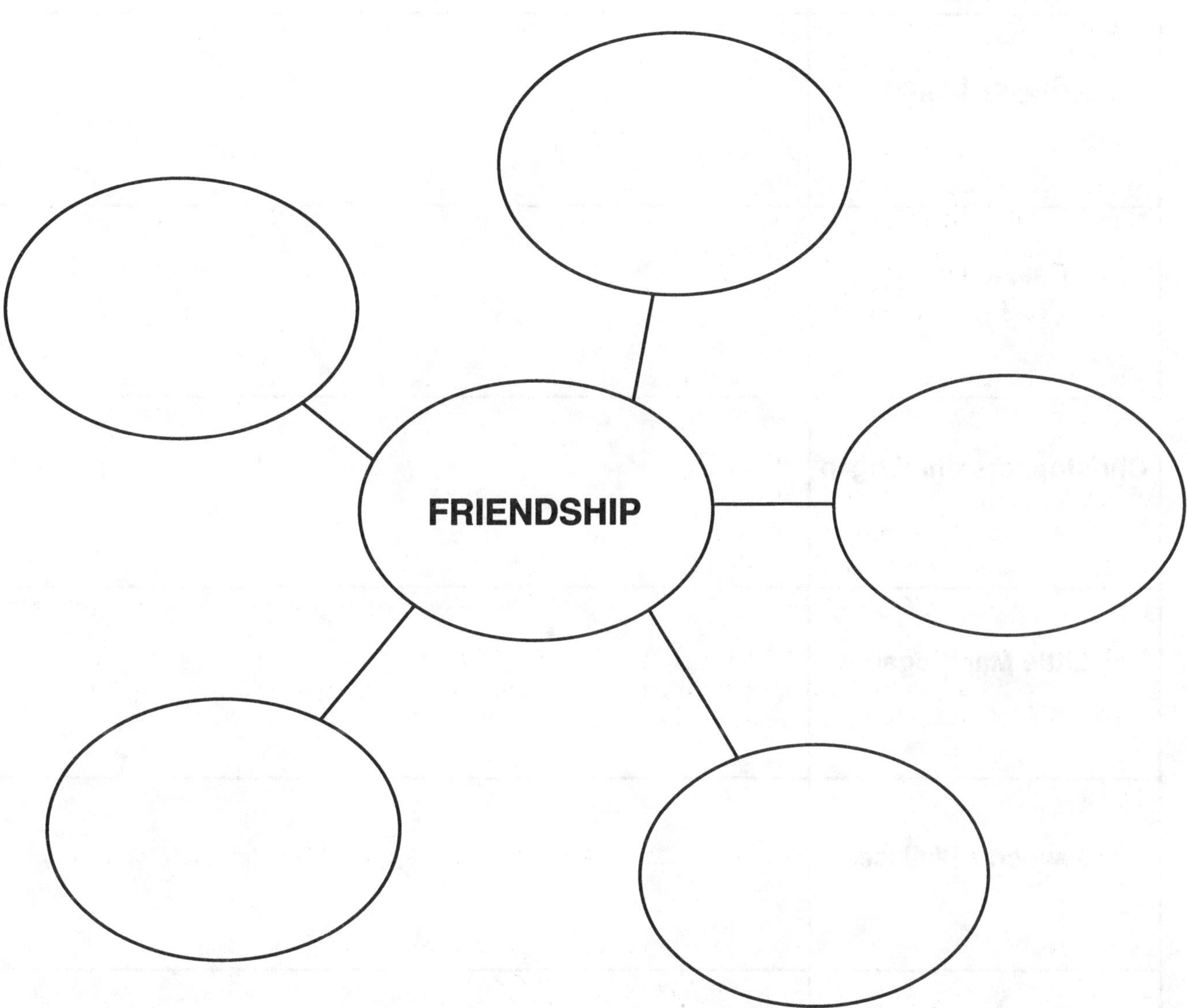

After reviewing your web, what are some of the basic ideas that express what friendship means to you?

____

____

____

____

Reaction Chart

"The Friendship" ends with the shooting of Mr. Tom Bee. The reader does not know what each character's reaction is to the shooting. Using the reaction chart below, predict how each character may have reacted to Mr. Tom Bee being shot.

Character	Reaction
Stacey Logan	
Cassie Logan	
Christopher-John Logan	
Little Man Logan	
Dewberry Wallace	
Jeremy	
Mr. Simms	

Aunt Flossie's Hats
(And Crab Cakes Later)

Author: Elizabeth Fitzgerald Howard

Illustrator: James Ransome

Publisher: Clarion, New York, 1991. 31 pages

Summary: Sarah and Susan love to go to Aunt Flossie's house and hear stories about days long gone as they try on her very special hats.

Background Information on African-Americans:

Almost all African-Americans living in the United States are descendants of slaves. Today, African-Americans comprise 12.5% of the total United States population. In 1990 there were 29,986,060 African-Americans living in the United States. Almost half of that number live in the southern and southeast states.

Connecting Activities:

- Flossie tells the girls a story about a terrible fire in Baltimore. Have students write a news report describing the details of the fire.

- Flossie tells the girls another story about a parade she attended upon conclusion of the war. Have students make signs announcing the parade. They can use construction paper to design their posters, then attach the posters to craft sticks.

- A very special dog, Gretchen, saved one of Flossie's favorite hats from going down the river. Have students make a thank-you card from Flossie to Gretchen or her owner.

- Flossie has a story to go with every one of her hats. Have students bring pieces of clothing to school and tell special stories about each piece.

- Allow students to make special hats adorned with ribbons, flowers, or feathers. Small straw hats can be purchased at craft stores fairly inexpensively and students can bring in the supplies they would like to use to decorate the hat. Then have them write special stories to go along with the hats they have designed.

In the Year of the Boar and Jackie Robinson

Author: Bette Bao Lord

Illustrator: Marc Simont

Publisher: HarperCollins, New York, 1984. 169 pages

Summary: Shirley Temple Wong is nervous about attending school in America. She has recently moved to America from China along with her parents and does not know anything about the culture. However, she soon begins to feel more at home when she becomes a real fan of baseball and Jackie Robinson.

Background Information on Chinese-Americans:

The California gold rush created the initial wave of immigrants from China. Now there are over 1.6 million Chinese-Americans living in the United States. You can find clusters of Chinese-Americans and markets in "Chinatowns" located in many major cities such as San Francisco, Los Angeles, and New York.

Connecting Activities:

(Chapters 1-3)

- Have students locate China on the Asia map located on page 30.

- Have students research to find out what year the current year is according to the Chinese calendar.

- In Shirley's culture, to have a bad dream on the night of New Year's Eve is considered a bad omen. Ask students whether they believe in any omens or superstitions.

- At the New Year's celebration everyone gets really dressed up. The dresses are often made of bright silk with gold and silver threads and adorned with sequins and pearls. Allow students to draw what they think these dresses may have looked like. Then they can add gold and silver glitter and small sequins, if they like.

In the Year of the Boar and Jackie Robinson (cont.)

- Shirley wants to adopt an "American" name when she finds out that she is moving. Apparently, she does not think Sixth Cousin is an appropriate name. So, she chooses Shirley Temple Wong. Ask students what celebrity names they would choose if they were allowed to change their names and why they would choose those names.

- It is very difficult for Shirley's mom to leave her family. Have students write diary entries for Shirley's mom describing her feelings on the day of their departure.

- Have students brainstorm and discuss the reasons why Shirley's parents show little affection toward each other upon their reunion.

- Have students draw pictures of typical cities in China and New York City, Shirley's new home. They can be encouraged to use reference books to help gain the background knowledge necessary to draw the pictures with accuracy. Then have students discuss the main differences between the two locations.

- Have students write letters from Shirley to Fourth Cousin describing her first day in Brooklyn.

- Shirley is afraid of starting school. Fortunately, the students in her class really try to make her feel welcome on her first day. Have students brainstorm ways they can make new students feel more welcome in your school and classroom. Students can make notes of their ideas on the activity sheet on page 94. As an extension activity students could also be asked to create a welcome folder for new students.

(Chapters 4-6)

- Allow students to play the ball game described on page 53 of *In The Year of the Boar and Jackie Robinson* during their physical education class.

- One of Shirley's favorite American snacks is cupcakes. Allow students to make cupcakes from a box mix.

- Shirley is having all sorts of different feelings about being in the United States. Sometimes she feels very alone because she is the only Chinese girl in her school. Have students write poems to describe Shirley's feelings about being in the United States.

In the Year of the Boar and Jackie Robinson *(cont.)*

- To help cheer up Shirley, her father buys her a brand new pair of shiny roller skates. Shirley is not very good at skating at first. So, her father offers to go skating with her, but Shirley is vehemently opposed to the idea. Have students discuss why Shirley wants to learn to skate on her own.

- When Shirley stands up to the toughest girl at school, she ends up with two black eyes. Have students write Shirley a letter offering advice for dealing with a "bully."

- Have students discuss in small groups why Mabel would want to be friends with Shirley after beating her up.

- Shirley is becoming very interested in baseball. Allow students to play baseball during their next few physical education classes.

- Shirley's grandfather once told her, "Things are not what they seem. Good can be bad. Bad can be good." Have students write an essay describing what they think Shirley's grandfather meant. Then have them offer situations in which something bad can be good and something good can be bad.

- Allow students to make posters for their favorite baseball team.

- Have students write biographies for Jackie Robinson or any other sports heroes. To assist them in collecting data, give them a copy of the activity sheet on page 95.

(Chapters 7–9)

- Shirley decides that during her summer vacation she will read books, sleep late, and listen to baseball games. Have students make lists of the things they like to do best during their vacation time.

- When Shirley finds out that Señora Rodriguez desperately wants to visit her daughter Nonnie, she volunteers her family to watch the apartment and the Señora's pet bird. Have students discuss in small groups whether or not they think Shirley should have volunteered her family for this job.

- Shirley constantly reads the sports section of the *Herald Tribune* to find out how the Dodgers are doing. Have students do current event reports for the next few weeks, focusing on sporting events.

In the Year of the Boar and Jackie Robinson (cont.)

- Shirley has a nightmare about her family in China that really frightens her. Have students write about scary nightmares they have had in their lives.

(Chapters 10-12)

- Shirley is immensely disappointed when the Dodgers lose the World Series. Have students imagine that they are good friends of Shirley's. Then have them write her letters describing times when they were really disappointed about something and how they dealt with these times.

- When the Chinese celebrate the brightest moon, they often hang paper lanterns. Allow students to make paper lanterns by following the directions below.

Materials: a rectangular piece of colored construction paper, a ruler, a pencil, scissors, and glue

1. Fold the construction paper in half lengthwise.

2. Begin at the center of the fold and draw a series of lines about ¾ of an inch (1.9 cm) apart. Leave about one inch (2.5 cm) of paper at the top and bottom edges of the paper.

3. Cut along the lines.

4. Glue the two sides of the paper together. Then, open the paper to form a lantern.

5. For a handle, glue a one-inch (2.5 cm) piece of construction paper to each side of the top of the lantern.

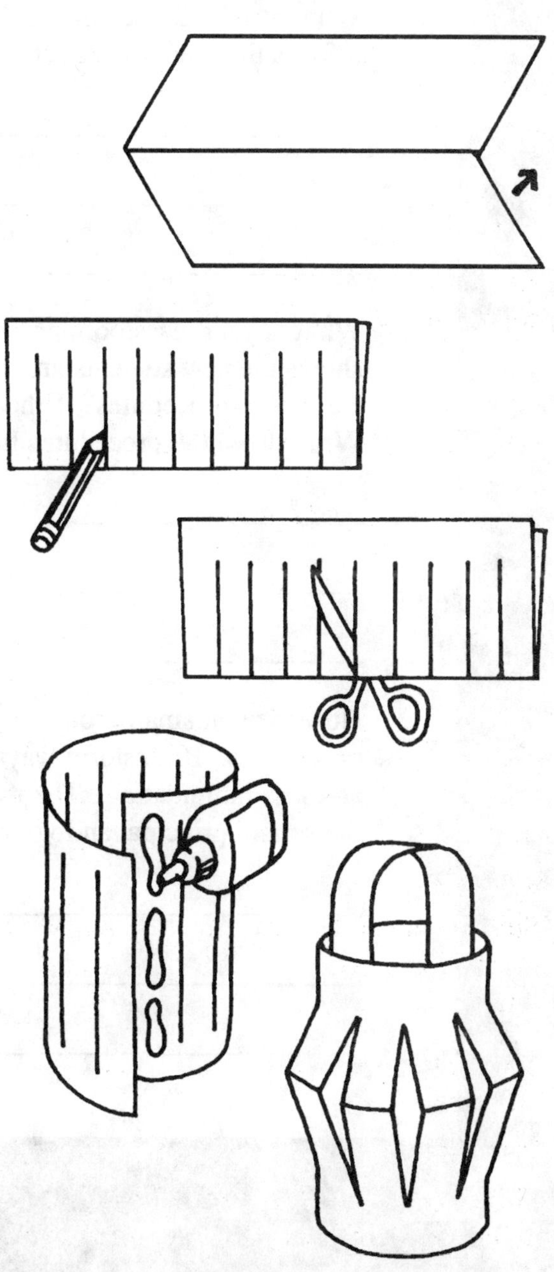

- On pages 152-154 of *In the Year of the Boar and Jackie Robinson* Shirley tells one of her grandfather's stories. Have students write an essay describing what they think the story means.

- Shirley is given the honor of introducing Jackie Robinson at her school. Have students write introductory speeches for Shirley to give.

- Shirley explains to Jackie Robinson that she can never be president of the United States because she was not born here. Have students discuss and debate whether or not they think this is fair.

Welcome Wagon

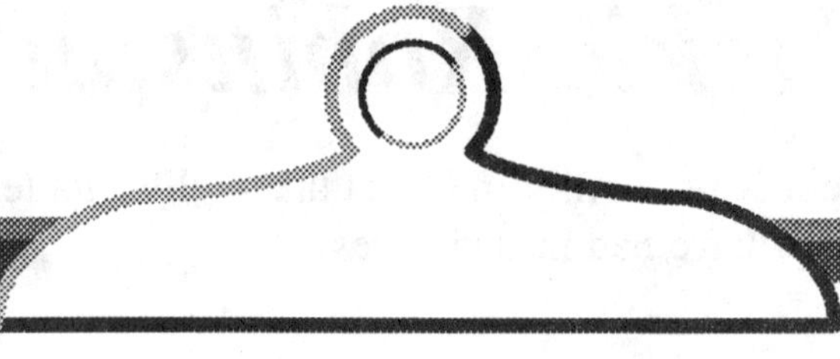

Shirley's class really tries to make her feel welcome on her first day. In this activity, you are asked to consider how your school and class can make new students feel comfortable.

1. Find out the school's policy for welcoming new students. Does someone show them around the school? What paperwork do they have to fill out? Who introduces the new student to the teacher? Write down the information about your school's policy below.

   ____

   ____

   ____

2. What is your classroom procedure for welcoming new students? Who shows the new students around at recess and lunch time? Who explains classroom procedures? Who helps to introduce the new student to people? Write down the procedures below.

   ____

   ____

   ____

3. Now meet in small groups to discuss the school and classroom policies and procedures. Brainstorm ways to make the first day for a new student easier and less intimidating. Then write your recommendations down to give to the school principal and your teacher.

   ____

   ____

   ____

Sports Hero Biography

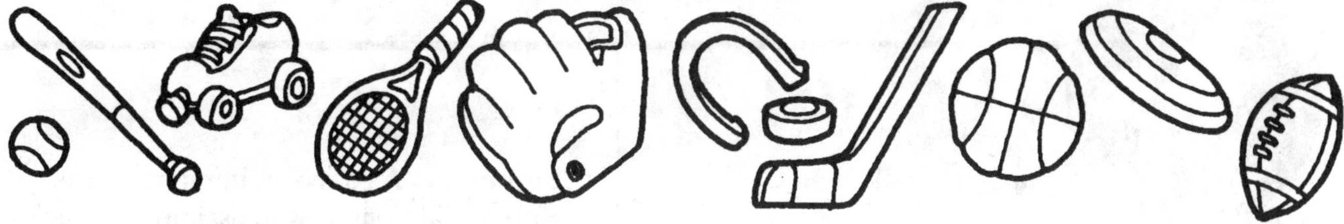

Use this activity sheet to help you conduct research for your sports hero biography.

1. Name of sports hero you will write a biography for: ___________________________

    ____

2. What is his/her sport? ____

3. What is his/her date of birth? ____

4. Where was he/she born? ____

5. Who are the other members of his/her family?_________________________________

    ____

6. When did he/she first became involved in the sport? ____________________________

    ____

7. Why did he/she become involved in the sport?_________________________________

    ____

8. Did he/she admire a certain hero of the sport? ________________________________

    ____

9. Did his/her parents encourage a career in professional sports? ____________________

10. What are some of the highlights of his/her career?______________________________

    ____

    ____

11. What do you think is the best characteristic of this sports hero? ___________________

    ____

    ____

Halmoni and the Picnic

Author: Sook Nyul Choi

Illustrator: Karen M. Dugan

Publisher: Houghton Mifflin, Boston, 1993. 31 pages

Summary: As a recent immigrant from Korea, Halmoni tries to assimilate into the American culture.

Background Information:

The first Korean immigrants were students and political refugees of the 1880's. Large-scale immigration occurred in 1903 for work on the Hawaiian sugar plantations. In 1990 there were 798,849 Korean-Americans in the United States. They are considered more widely dispersed than any other Asian group.

Connecting Activities:

- Have students locate Korea on the Asia map on page 30.

- Halmoni does not understand American customs, including what is considered rude in the American culture. Have students make a list of ten things that are considered rude in the American culture.

- Have students write letters to Halmoni thanking her for attending their picnic. The letter can be from either a student or the teacher, Mrs. Nolan.

- Have students each make a list of five things they eat that may seem odd to a foreigner.

- Challenge students to find out how to say mother, father, and grandfather in Korean.

- Allow students to organize a special Grandparents' Day Picnic. Students could prepare special foods to bring to the picnic that day. Students can use the special invitation on page 97 to give to their grandparents.

A Special Invitation

Send the invitation below to your grandparents to announce the special Grandparents' Day Picnic. Color the invitation and write as neatly as possible.

Dear: _______________________

You are invited to attend a Grandparents' Day Picnic!

WHERE:

WHEN:

TIME:

OTHER IMPORTANT INFORMATION:

Too Many Tamales

Author: Gary Soto

Illustrator: Ed Martinez

Publisher: Putnam, New York, 1993. 28 pages

Summary: Maria enjoys helping her mother make tamales for Christmas. However, when Maria fears that she has accidentally lost her mother's ring in one of the tamales, she worries that it will not be a happy holiday.

Background Information on Mexican-Americans:

Since World War II, Mexico has been the source of the largest number of legal immigrants coming to the United States. The total number of Mexican-Americans living in the United States in 1990 was 12,110,000. They tend to concentrate in large urban areas in Texas, New Mexico, Arizona, and Southern California.

Connecting Activities:

- Have students locate Mexico on the North America map on page 124.

- Maria enjoys helping her mother make tamales for the holiday dinner. Have students share stories about times when they helped parents with something special.

- Maria should not try on her mother's ring without permission. Have students write about times when they did something they were not supposed to do and what happened as a result.

- The children enjoy cutting out pictures of toys they would like to receive for Christmas. Allow students to look through catalogs, magazines, and newspapers and cut out items they would like to receive as gifts. They can glue these to construction paper, along with drawings of other items they would like.

- When Maria realized that her mother's ring must be inside one of the tamales, she suggested that the children eat them all to find it. Have students brainstorm other ways Maria could have handled the situation.

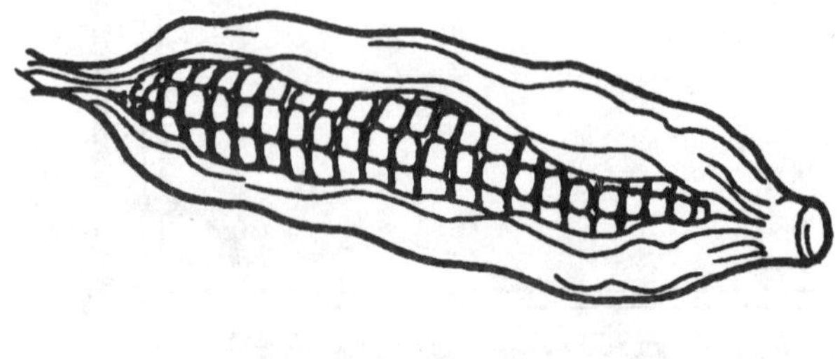

Taking Sides

Author: Gary Soto

Publisher: Harcourt, Brace, and Company, New York, 1991. 135 pages

Summary: When Lincoln Mendoza and his mother move from the barrio to the suburbs they face many changes. Will Lincoln accept his new lifestyle or long to return to his old buddies of the barrio?

Background Information on Mexican-Americans:

See the information on page 98.

Connecting Activities:

(Chapters 1-3)

- Have students locate Mexico on the North America map on page 124.

- Lincoln's mother decides to move away from the barrio after coming home to find that her home has been burglarized. Have students imagine that they work for the police department. It is their job to write up police reports for the burglary and create a wanted poster.

- Lincoln's mother, Beatrice, is a graphic artist and owns her own advertising business. Her top clients are six computer companies. Have students create an advertising campaign for a computer product or company.

- Lincoln's friend, Monica, has to write every day in a journal for school. Ask students to write a one-page journal entry every day for one week. You may choose to specify the type of entries they should include or simply make it a free-writing exercise.

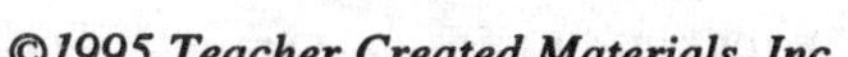

- Lincoln lives in Northern California and his father lives in Southern California. They communicate infrequently by writing letters. Have students write letters as either Lincoln describing his new neighborhood or as his father describing recent events in his own life. Students will have to use their imaginations regarding Lincoln's father's life because there is little information provided in the book.

Taking Sides (cont.)

- Lincoln thinks the basketball team at his new school is like the Lakers and the team from his old school is like the Warriors, a much less successful team. Ask students to think about an athletic team at your school. To what professional team would they compare the school team to and why?

- Lincoln and his mother often eat frijoles and papas for dinner. Allow students to eat beans and potatoes for lunch one day.

(Chapters 4-6)

- Lincoln really does not like his mother's boyfriend Roy. Consequently, when he is invited to go to dinner with Beatrice and Roy, he makes up an excuse not to attend. Ask students what they would advise Lincoln to do. Is refusing to go disrespectful?

- Lincoln and his mother speak English at home. Now that Lincoln has fewer opportunities to speak Spanish, he is forgetting his native language. Ask students whether they think it is important for Lincoln to maintain his first language.

- Lincoln enjoys visiting his friend Tony. Tony's mother is a very kind lady and often gets kept on the phone by sales people because she does not want to be rude. Have students brainstorm polite ways to deal with unwanted phone calls.

- When Lincoln visits Tony after his move, he realizes that he may be changing somewhat. Have students make a list of ways in which they think Lincoln has changed since he moved away from the barrio. Then ask them to comment on whether or not they think these changes are good ones.

- Lincoln and Tony get into a fight during their visit together. Have students discuss in small groups whether or not they think Lincoln treated Tony improperly.

(Chapters 7-10)

- Beatrice sometimes becomes frustrated with Lincoln because she feels he does not contribute to the household in any way. Ask students to consider the ways in which they contribute at their own homes. Ask them to make lists of their contributions. Then ask them to make lists of other ways they could help out at home.

Taking Sides (cont.)

- Beatrice will not let Lincoln have Nintendo because she thinks it is violent. Have students write a position statement on whether or not they feel some Nintendo games are violent and what should be done about it.

- Allow students to play any of the basketball games Lincoln enjoys playing: Around the World, Horse, or Twenty-One.

- Lincoln and Monica are both former students of Franklin Junior High. Now, however, they should be loyal students of their new school, Columbus. Take a class vote to see which side the students in your class think Lincoln and Monica will take for the big game.

- When Lincoln finds out that Roy once played basketball with his current coach, Lincoln becomes more interested in Roy. It turns out that they have more in common than Lincoln ever thought. Have students write a conversation that could occur between Lincoln and his mother wherein Lincoln explains that he may have been wrong about his earlier opinions of Roy.

- Both schools, Franklin and Columbus, are described in detail throughout the book. Have students complete the comparison chart for the two schools on page 102.

- Lincoln eats deer meat when visiting a friend. When he tells his friend Monica about this, she is repulsed. Have students debate their own feelings about eating deer meat or any other kind of meat.

(Chapters 11-13)

- When Roy thinks Lincoln is being mistreated by the coach, he says he will go to the game and "straighten him out." Have students write letters to Lincoln offering advice on how to handle his difficulty with the coach. Should Roy be asked to intervene?

- Prior to the start of the big game, the coach makes a speech about school tradition and spirit. Have students write speeches for the coach to give to the team.

- Allow students to make up cheers for either of the teams.

- The story ends with Lincoln on the phone to Monica. He has some things he wants to tell her. Have students write the conversation they think took place between Monica and Lincoln.

Comparison Chart

Use the chart below to note differences between the two junior high schools that Lincoln attended, Franklin and Columbus. Consider the types of classes offered, number of students, socio-economic status of the students at each school, and athletic ability, to name just a few topics. When you have completed the charts, answer the questions that follow. You can write your answers on the back of this page.

Franklin	**Columbus**

1. What do you think is the biggest difference between the two schools?

____

____

2. To which school would you rather go and why?

____

____

Maybe I Will Do Something

Author: Wayne Ude

Illustrator: Abigail Rorer

Publisher: Houghton Mifflin, 1993. 68 pages

Summary: Seven stories involving a coyote and other wild creatures explain the beginning of the world.

Background Information on Native Americans:

It has been alleged that the ancestors of Native American people arrived in America more than 20,000 years ago. Today, the total number of Native Americans living in the United States is 1.9 million (1990). One-half of the Native Americans live on some 300 reservations located in Arizona, New Mexico, Utah, South Dakota, Montana, and Washington. The other half live in cities in the north, central, western states, and in Alaska.

Connecting Activities:

(Chapters 1-2)

- In the first chapter the author suggests that coyotes have special powers. Have students discuss in small groups whether or not they think coyotes have any special powers as the first story suggests.

- Coyote and Wolf have a tenuous relationship at best. After reading chapter one, ask students whether they think Coyote and Wolf will remain friends.

- Coyote loves beautiful sunsets. Have students draw a picture with Coyote in the foreground and a beautiful sunset in the background.

- Have students discuss why they think the Sun gave the Coyote the special leggings.

Maybe I Will Do Something (cont.)

- The coyote and wolf begin the story on a raft in the ocean. They meet several oceanic creatures while on the raft. Allow students to create a crayon resist seascape of what the coyote and wolf may have seen while on the raft.

Materials: construction paper, crayons, watercolor paints, and paintbrush

1. Draw a seascape on a piece of construction paper using crayons.

2. Lightly paint over the picture with blue watercolor paint.

3. Allow to dry. Then, hang the pictures in the classroom.

- Copy the coyote picture on page 106 for each of your students. Have them color the coyotes, then as a class draw and color a large mural background for the coyotes. When the mural is complete, allow students to place their coyote pictures on the mural.

(Chapters 3-4)

- In each of the stories the animals talk to each other. Have students discuss in small groups whether or not they think animals can speak to each other. Also, have them discuss the ways in which people and animals communicate with each other. You may suggest they use specific examples from experiences with their own pets.

- Have students write journal entries to respond to this question: Why is having power dangerous if you are not responsible? Encourage the use of examples from the story for their responses.

- Ask students how the story, "Coyote Learns a Lesson", relates to the Indian notion of taking from the earth only what you need.

Maybe I Will Do Something (cont.)

(Chapters 5-7)

- Have students explore the idea of extinction of animals. Ask them what would happen if the very last buffalo were killed or if only weak buffalo were left to survive. Then have them research which animals are currently at risk of extinction.

- Have students imagine that Coyote is a human being. Then have them create personality profiles for Coyote. Would they want to be Coyote's friend? Why or why not?

- As a class, discuss whether or not students think Coyote will ever get his eyes back.

- Have students research the differences between coyotes and wolves. Then have them write brief reports of their findings.

- Coyote has many self-esteem problems. So, he is devastated when the other animals laugh at him. Have students write descriptive pieces about the way Coyote must have felt when everyone began laughing at him.

- As a class, brainstorm why the circle is often considered a "holy" shape.

- Coyote loves eating berries in the wild. Allow students to enjoy eating fresh berries in class.

- In the afterword of *Maybe I Will Do Something*, the author describes the Coyote stories as "trickster tales." He also states that the Coyote stories are not the only trickster tales. Have students research other animal trickster tales. Then have them share some of the stories they found with the rest of the class. You may also suggest that students share some of the stories with other classes that may be studying Native Americans.

- Now that students have read all the stories, challenge them to identify the lesson in each story.

Coyote Pattern

Color and cut the coyote pattern below. Then, place it on a classroom background mural of the environment in which coyotes live.

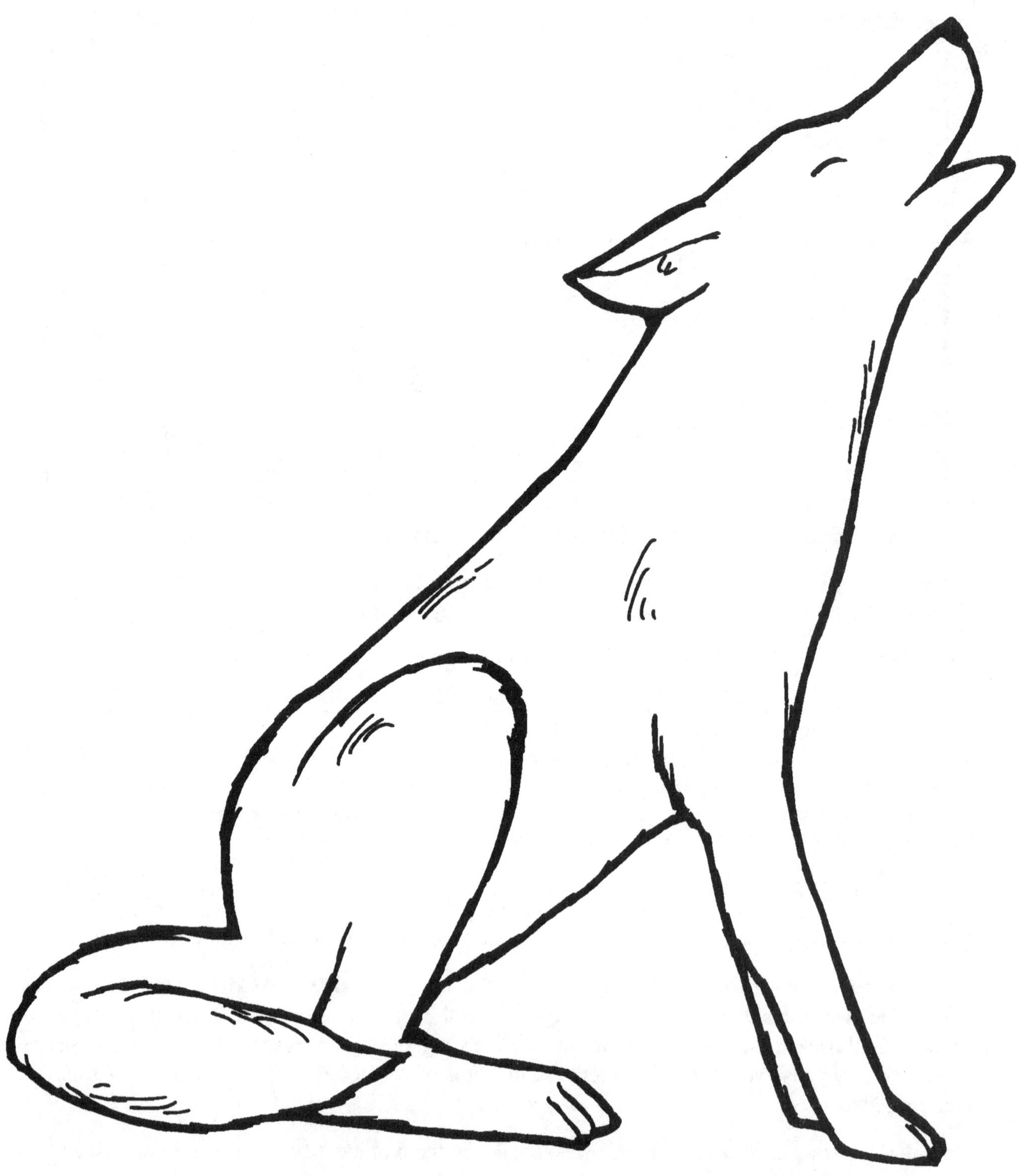

The Light in the Forest

Author: Conrad Richter

Publisher: Bantam, New York, 1953. 117 pages

Summary: At a young age True Son is adopted into the Indian culture. When he is a teenager and returned to his real parents, True Son decides he wants to remain with the Indians.

Background Information on Native Americans:

See background information located on page 103.

Connecting Activities:

(Chapters 1-4)

- Have students discuss whether they think that whites who are not prisoners and want to remain with the Indians should be forced to be returned.

- Have students predict what happened to True Son's real parents.

- Have students create a "missing" poster designed by True Son's real parents in an effort to find him.

- Ask students to write about what they think True Son meant when he said he wanted to go to "a place where you can't tramp me with your big foot."

- Have students draw and describe an item that makes them feel like they are at home.

- Have students write a special farewell message from True Son to his Indian father.

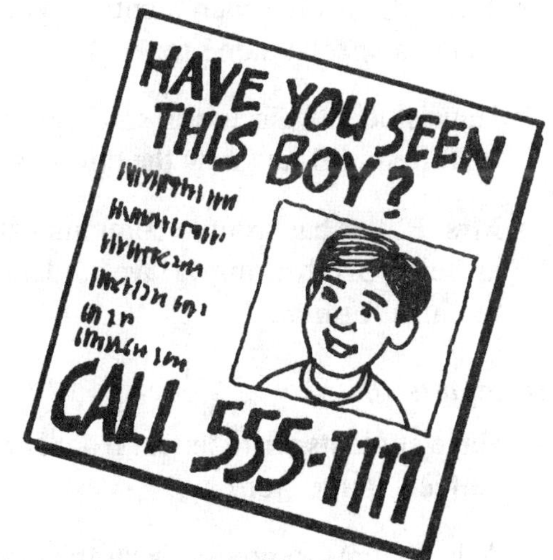

(Chapters 5-9)

- Have students imagine themselves as True Son being interviewed by a psychologist. Then, have them respond in writing as to why True Son loathes his own white people.

The Light in the Forest *(cont.)*

- True Son probably has many expectations about his real family. Using the activity sheet on page 109, have students record what they think True Son's expectations are.

- As a class, have students brainstorm how Mrs. Butler could have better handled True Son's arrival.

- In small groups, have students discuss the relationship between Gordie and True Son. Why do they think the two brothers get along so well?

- Have students draw two pictures of True Son, one in his Indian clothes and one in the clothes his mother wants him to wear.

- The Indians give each month a special name. Using the activity sheet on page 110, have students create a special name for each month.

- Have students discuss in small groups whether they think True Son's opinion of the Indians would be different if he knew the circumstances surrounding his initial disappearance.

- Mrs. Butler has trouble communicating her feelings to True Son. Consequently, she often comes off as being overbearing. Have students write letters from Mrs. Butler to True Son describing her feelings for him.

(Chapters 10-15)

- Have students write letters from Mr. Butler to True Son, attempting to resolve the burden and guilt he feels in the story.

- Ask students to predict what they think is making True Son so sick.

- Ask students to discuss what True Son's real parents could possibly do to make him want to stay.

- Have students write letters from True Son to his real parents, explaining why he does not feel he can stay with them.

- Allow students to play the black and white stone game described on page 99 of *The Light in the Forest.*

- Have students predict what will become of True Son now that he has no home.

Great Expectations

True Son must have had many expectations upon his arrival to meet his real parents. Predict his expectations for his mother, father, and brother in the boxes below.

Mother

Father

Brother

Creative Names for the Months of the Year

The Indians gave a special name to each month. For example, January is called the Month When the Ground Squirrels Begin to Run. Use your creative imagination to make up new names for each month of the year.

January	February	March
April	**May**	**June**
July	**August**	**September**
October	**November**	**December**

Meet Kirsten

Author: Janet Shaw

Illustrator: Renee Graef

Publisher: Pleasant Company, 1986. 61 pages

Summary: This book is part of the American Girls Series and describes Kirsten's difficult journey to the United States and then to Minnesota.

Connecting Activities:

Chapters 1-3

- Challenge students to make a rag doll like the one Kirsten treasures.

- Invite students to donate apples, cherries, and bread. Then, have a feast with the types of food Kirsten often ate.

- Many people on the journey died of typhoid and cholera. Divide the class in two groups. Ask each group to research one of the diseases. What are the symptoms? Do these diseases still exist? Are they still fatal?

- Ask students if they have ever been lost. Then, have them write a story about the event. If they have never been lost ask them to make up a story and use their imaginations to describe what being lost would be like.

- Have students write a thank you letter from Kirsten to the lady who helped her find her family.

- Have students write a letter from Kirsten to her grandmother describing their trip.

Chapters 4-5 (also *"Looking Back"*)

- Have students write a diary entry by Kirsten regarding Marta's death.

- Ask students to draw the house Kirsten's family saw in the distance.

- Kirsten and her cousins have their own secret club. Ask students to create their own secret club. Ask them to write the purpose of their club.

- Have students answer the questions in "Looking Back."

- In a previous activity, students created their own club. For this activity students will write the rules for the club they created. They may use the activity sheet on page 112. Then, have students make a list of rules for Kirsten's club using page 113. On a separate piece of paper students can compare the two sets of rules and discuss why they are different.

Meet Kirsten (cont.)

Make a list of rules for the club you created.

Name: _______________________________

My Club Rules

Meet Kirsten (cont.)

Make a list of rules Kirsten and her cousins may have had for their club.

Name: _______________________________

Kirsten's Rules

____

____

____

____

____

____

____

____

____

____

____

____

____

____

____

____

Shadow of the Dragon

Author: Sherry Garland

Publisher: Harcourt, Brace, and Company, New York, 1993. 314 pages

Summary: Danny has settled into American life and enjoys high school and his close friends. However, when his cousin arrives from Hong Kong after being in a re-education camp for many years, Danny's life becomes more complicated.

Background Information:

Vietnamese-Americans, along with Cambodian-Americans and Laotian-Americans, are generally all considered part of the group called Southeast Asian immigrants. Initially, most of these immigrants came to the United States to flee Vietnam in 1975. Southeast Asian immigrants number more than one million (1990) and generally live in California, Texas, New York, and Pennsylvania.

Connecting Activities:

(Chapters 1-2)

- Have students locate Vietnam on the Asia map on page 30.

- Danny was born in the Year of the Dragon, which is considered the luckiest sign in the Vietnamese zodiac. Have half the class research the Vietnamese zodiac and half the class research the American zodiac. Then, have them compare the two.

- Danny is often accused of being part of the Vietcong. Have students research who and what the Vietcong was. Discuss the Vietcong in terms of the Vietnam War to provide background information for the book.

- Danny is nice enough to save two young Vietnamese girls from the Cobra gang. Have students write letters to Danny from either one of the girls, thanking him for his help and bravery.

Shadow of the Dragon *(cont.)*

- Tet is the name of the Vietnamese New Year. For the Vietnamese this is the most important event of the year. Vietnamese people who no longer live in Vietnam try to reproduce as many of the traditions as possible. The Vietnamese decorate their houses with plum blossoms for the New Year. Allow students to make decorative blossoms by following the directions below.

Materials: bare branches, crepe paper or tissue paper, scissors, a pencil, and glue

1. Cut small squares of crepe or tissue paper.
2. Wrap a square of tissue or crepe paper around the eraser tip of the pencil. Dip the end in glue.
3. Place the tissue paper randomly on the branch.
4. Decorate the classroom with the colorful branches.

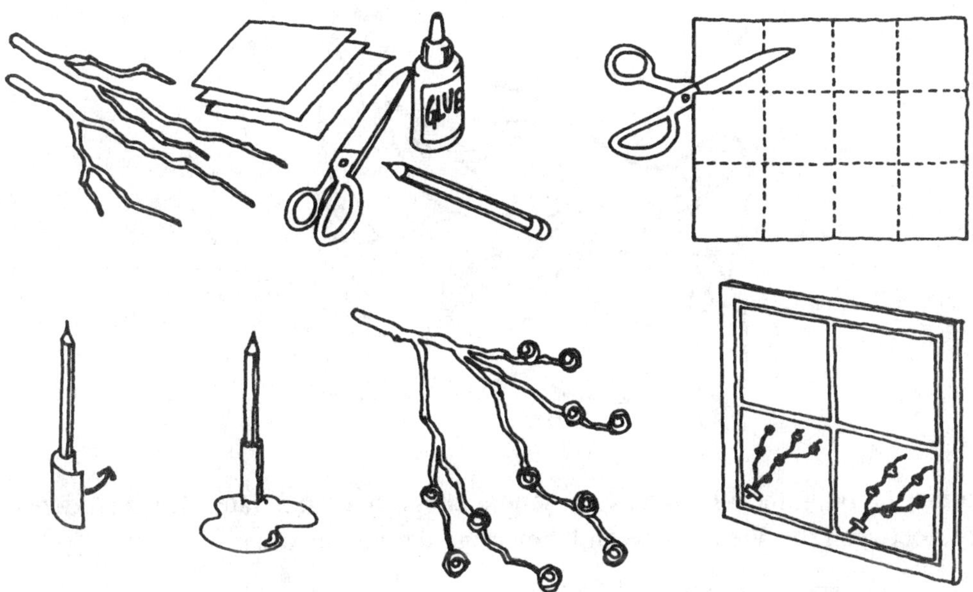

- Jasmine tea is popular among the Vietnamese. Allow students to have jasmine tea.

- Have students predict what might have happened to the girls if Danny had not stepped in when he did.

- Danny has extra responsibilities because he is the oldest in his family. Have students interview students to find out whether they have certain responsibilities based on their birth order. They can use the activity sheet on page 119 to record the data they acquire.

- In small groups, have students discuss whether or not they think junior high students should be allowed to dress as they like if they pay for the clothes themselves.

- Danny's grandma, or Ba, tells his younger sister that family is more important than friends. Have students write essays responding to this statement.

- Danny's family plans a big party to welcome Sang Le into their home and family. Have students make lists of things they would do to make visiting relatives feel welcome in their homes.

- Have students predict how well Sang Le will fit into the family.

Shadow of the Dragon (cont.)

(Chapters 3-4)

- Have students write poems about freedom from Sang Le's point of view.

- Have students research what is happening in Vietnam today. They can use the activity sheet on page 120.

- Have students write fairy tales about an emperor or dragon.

- Danny knew that his life would be changed by the arrival of his cousin. Have students record their predictions of the ways in which Danny's life will change.

- Have students draw dragons for Danny.

- It is customary among the Vietnamese to send a chaperone on a date. Have students discuss the differences between the Vietnamese and American dating customs.

- Sang Le loves the Vietnamese love songs from his country. Danny, however, does not appreciate that music. Have students discuss current popular songs. Then, make a class graph to represent the types of music your students enjoy most.

- Have students write letters of advice to Kim about becoming involved with a brother of someone who is in the Cobra gang.

- Sang Le dreams about his bad memories. Have students draw pictures representing what they think Sang Le sees in his bad dreams.

(Chapters 5-7)

- Have students write letters to friends in Vietnam from Sang Le, describing what it is like living in America.

- Sang Le believes you should marry only someone from your own culture. Have students discuss what they think of this philosophy.

- The Vietnamese New Year is a very important holiday. Have students describe in writing their favorite holidays in their own cultures. Then, have them glue their descriptions to one-half of a piece of construction paper and on the other half glue pictures of a family holiday celebration.

Shadow of the Dragon (cont.)

- The first visitor of the New Year is very important to the Vietnamese. Have students write about who they would choose to be their first visitors and why.

- As a class, discuss whether people can be misjudged based on their appearances. Encourage students to offer examples for this based on personal experience or perhaps news stories they have read or heard.

- Have students write biographies for Tho. They will have to use their imaginations to fill in many details of his life, but they should have a general idea based on the information given in the book.

(Chapters 8-10)

- Danny is unable to get a job he really wants because he is not yet sixteen years old. Sang Le offers to work for half pay because he cannot speak good English. However, because of the minimum wage law, he cannot be hired. Ask students to write letters to their congressman, supporting or arguing against these laws.

- When Danny suspects Sang Le might be getting involved with a gang, he wonders whether or not he should confront Sang Le. Have students write letters of advice to Danny about what they think he should do.

- As a class, discuss the ways in which Danny can stop Sang Le before he becomes too involved with the gang. Then have students write essays describing what they would do if they found out a friend was about to join a gang.

- Invite a local law enforcement officer to the class to talk about gangs.

- Sang Le is an incredible artist. He draws watercolor pictures of his country. Allow students to use watercolors to paint one of their favorite places.

- When Danny and Tiffany go to the Vietnamese restaurant she tries to use chopsticks. Challenge students to try to use chopsticks to eat their lunches. For an extra challenge, make rice for students to attempt to eat with the chopsticks.

- Have students write diary entries for either Danny or Tiffany describing their first date.

- Allow students to use the special border on page 121 to create special invitations for Dao's and Lien's baby's first birthday party.

Shadow of the Dragon (cont.)

- It is a Vietnamese custom to place several objects in front of babies to see which they choose. The objects the babies choose determine their futures. Dao's and Lien's baby chooses the rose, which means she will be a flirt. Have students make lists of what the other items may mean for the future. The other items include: a comb, scissors, pen, ruler, coin, and clod of dirt.

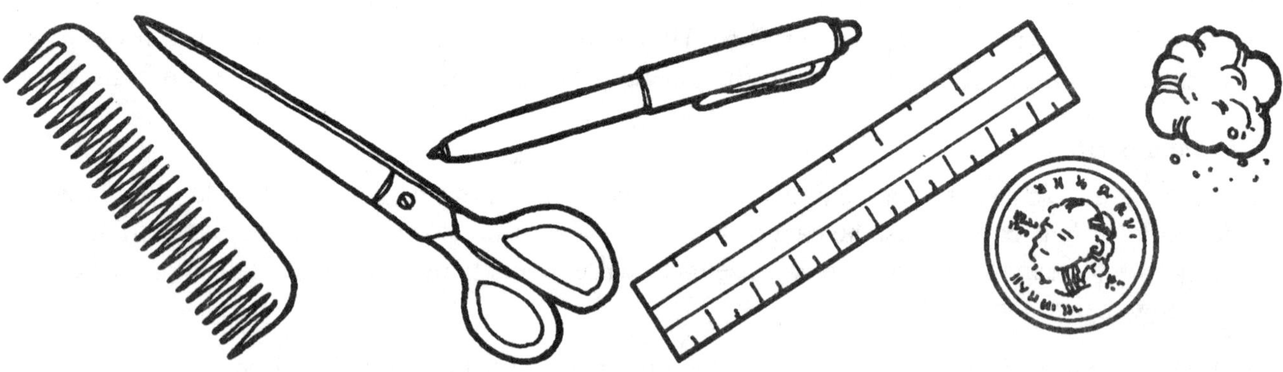

- Have students discuss whether or not they think Danny has a right to pressure Tiffany to tell Frank about their relationship.

(Chapters 11-14)

- Have students discuss the reasons why Kim may have run away. Then have them research the top three reasons teenagers run away in this country. Ask them to consider ways to prevent teenage runaways.

- Have students prepare speeches about gangs based on what they have read in the story. Their speech should be written to dissuade students from joining gangs.

- When Danny takes Tiffany dancing, they hear a song that is very meaningful to him. Ask students to write down the lyrics of songs that are powerful to them for some reason. Then ask them to explain the lyrics and the personal connections they have to the lyrics.

- Have students discuss how Danny should handle the delicate situation with Tiffany's brother Frank.

- Danny and Sang Le play cards to pass the time. Allow students to play some of their favorite card games in small groups.

(Chapter 15 and the *Epilogue)*

- Have students write special tributes to Sang Le's life.

- Have students write their own reactions to Sang Le's death.

- Danny is not able to forgive Tiffany. Have students discuss how they think Sang Le would want Danny to treat Tiffany.

- Have students use the activity sheet on page 122 to record how they think each character will be affected by Sang Le's death.

Birth Order Study

Danny had certain responsibilities because he was the oldest child. Your task is to find out whether or not children in the United States have certain responsibilities based on their birth order. Interview other students who are either the oldest, youngest, or middle children. Try to have at least one interview with someone from each category. Then, record the responsibilities they have based on their birth orders. When your study is complete, share your findings with the rest of the class.

Oldest Child in the Family

Responsibilities: ____

____

____

____

____

____

Middle Child in the Family

Responsibilities: ____

____

____

____

____

____

Youngest Child in the Family

Responsibilities: ____

____

____

____

____

____

Vietnam Today

Conduct some research to find out what Vietnam is like today. Answer the first few statements, then record any additional relevant information you locate. At the bottom of the page is room for you to record any current events related to Vietnam.

Current population of Vietnam: _______________________________________

____

____

____

____

Current government: ____

____

____

____

Current difficulties facing the country: _______________________________

____

____

Current relationship with the United States: ___________________________

____

____

Current relationship with other neighboring countries: __________________

____

____

Other relevant information: ____

____

____

Current events relating to Vietnam: ___________________________________

____

Special Invitation

Use the special bordered paper below to create an invitation to the first birthday party of Dao's and Lien's baby. Remember what a big event the first birthday is in the Vietnamese culture.

Reaction Chart

Use this chart to record the reactions of the main characters to Sang Le's death. Then answer the question at the bottom of the page.

DANNY	BA

TIFFANY	KIM

DANNY'S MOTHER	DANNY'S FATHER

FRANK	HONG

Which character do you think will be hit the hardest and suffer the most because of Sang Le's death? Explain why.

____

____

____

____

____

North America Bibliography

African-American

Cameron, Ann. *Julian's Glorious Summer.* (Random House, 1987)
Hamilton, Virginia. *Cousins.* (Philomel, 1990)
Moore, Emily. *Something to Count On.* (Dutton, 1980)
Myers, Walter Dean. *Me, Mop, and the Moondance.* (Delacorte, 1988)
Strickland, Dorothy. *Listen Children: An Anthology of Black Literature.* (Bantam, 1982)
Taylor, Mildred. *Mississippi Bridge.* (Dial, 1990)
Walter, Mildred Pitts. *Mariah Keeps Cool.* (Bradbury, 1990)
Williams-Garcia, Rita. *Fast Talk on a Slow Track.* (Lodestar, 1991)
Yarbrough, Camille. *The Shimmershine Queens.* (Putnam, 1989)

Chinese-American

Bang, Molly. *The Paper Crane.* (Morrow, 1987)
Say, Allen. *El Chino.* (Houghton Mifflin, 1990)
Waters, Kate, & Madeline Slovenz-Low. *Lion Dancer: Ernie Wan's Chinese New Year.* (Scholastic, 1990)
Yen, Clara. *Why Rat Comes First.* (Children's Book Press, 1991)
Yep, Laurence. *The Rainbow People.* (Harper & Row, 1989)

Korean-American

McDonald, Joyce. *Mail-Order Kid.* (Putnam, 1988)
Rhee, Nami. *Magic Spring.* (Putnam, 1993)
Sobol, Harriet Langsam. *We Don't Look Like Our Mom and Dad.* (Coward-McCann, 1984)

Mexican-American

Hall, Mahji. *T Is for Terrific.* (Open Hand, 1989)
Hewett, Joan. *Laura Loves Horses.* (Clarion, 1990)
Hurwitz, Johanna. *Class President.* (William Morrow, 1990)
Lomas Garza, Carmen. *Family Pictures.* (Children's Book Press, 1990)
Mohr, Micholasa. *Going Home.* (Dial, 1986)
Williams, Vera B. *A Chair for My Mother.* (Greenwillow, 1982)
Williams, Vera B. *Music, Music for Everyone.* (Greenwillow, 1984)
Williams, Vera B. *Something Special for Me.* (Greenwillow, 1983)

Native-American

Bruchac, Joseph. *Fox Song.* (Philomel, 1993)
Carter, Forrest. *The Education of Little Tree.* (Delacorte, 1976)
Cooper, Michael. *Racing Sled Dogs.* (Houghton Mifflin, 1987)
Holling, H. *Tree in the Trail.* (Houghton Mifflin, 1942)
Hudson, Jan. *Sweetgrass.* (Philomel, 1989)
Jennes, Aylette, & Alice Rivers. *In Two Worlds: A Yup'ik Eskimo Family.* (Houghton Mifflin, 1989)
Lattimore, Deborah Nourse. *The Flame of Peace: A Tale of the Aztecs.* (Harper & Row, 1987)
Martin, Rafe. *The Rough-Face Girl.* (Putnam, 1992)
Monroe, Jean Guard, & Ray Williamson. *They Dance in the Sky.* (Houghton Mifflin, 1987)
Oughton, Jerrie. *How the Stars Fell Into the Sky.* (Houghton Mifflin, 1992)
Perrine, Mary. *Nannabah's Friend.* (Houghton Mifflin, 1970)
Turner, Bonnie. *The Haunted Igloo.* (Houghton Mifflin, 1991)
Wheeler, Bernelda. *Where Did You Get Your Moccasins?* (Pemmican, 1986)
Zola, Meguido, & Angela Dereume. *Nobody.* (Pemmican, 1983)

Vietnamese-American

Brown, Tricia. *Lee-Ann The Story of a Vietnamese-American Girl.* (Putnam, 1991)
Surat, Michele Maria. *Angel Child, Dragon Child.* (Raintree, 1983)

Japanese-American

Friedman, Ina R. *How My Parents Learned to Eat.* (Houghton Mifflin, 1984)
Uchida, Yoshiko. *The Best Bad Thing.* (Macmillan, 1983)
Uchida, Yoshiko. *A Jar of Dreams.* (Macmillan, 1981)

Map of North America

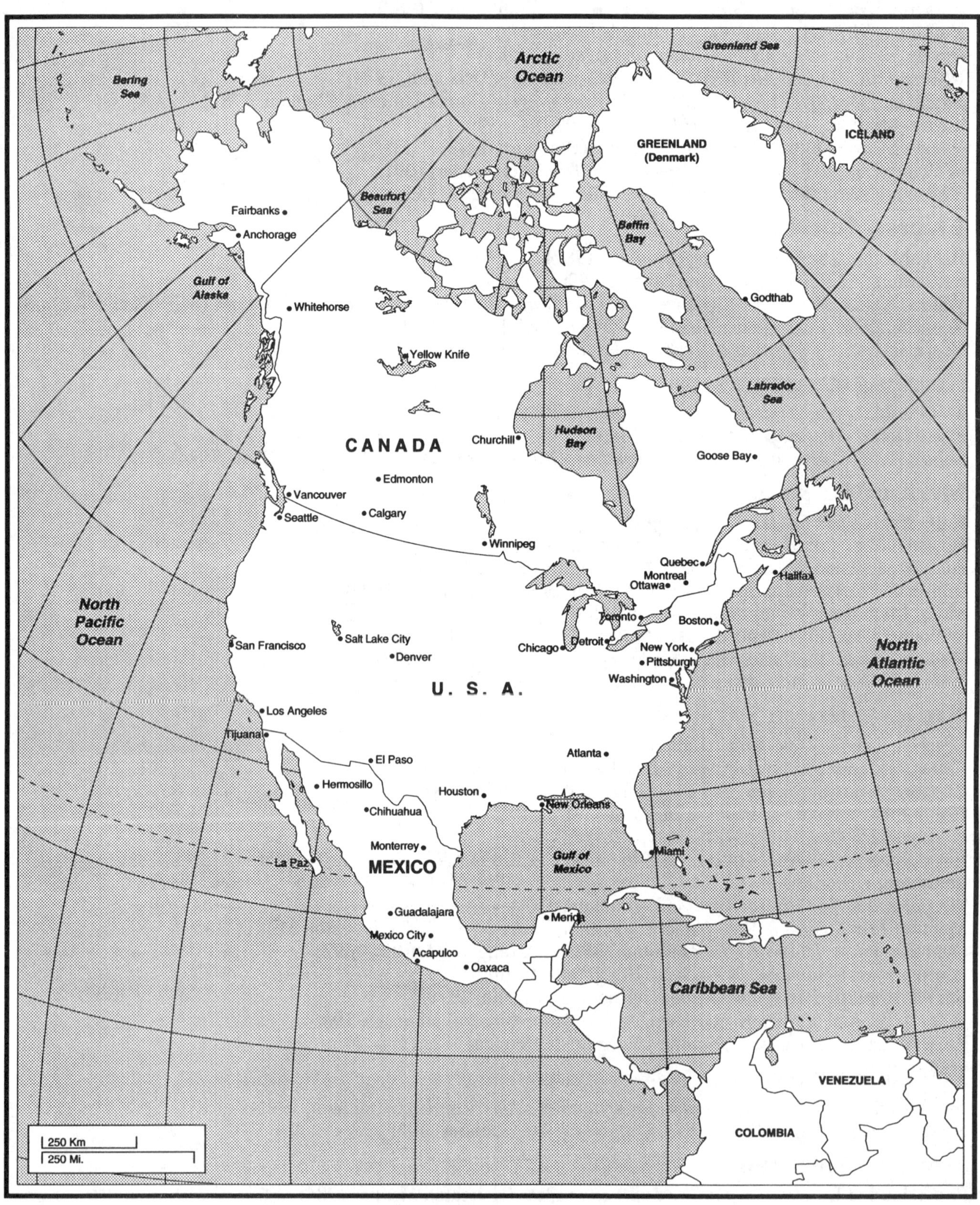

Where Angels Glide at Dawn

Editors: Lori M. Carlson and Cynthia L. Ventura

Illustrator: Jose Ortega

Publisher: HarperCollins, New York, 1990. 104 pages

Summary: A collection of multicultural stories is translated for students to enjoy.

Background Information:

This book is a collection of stories from Latin America. Latin America comprises Spanish and Portuguese speaking areas of the Western Hemisphere, including Mexico and most of Central and South America. Background information for each country is given below.

Argentina "The Bear's Speech"

Official Name: Argentina Republic

Area: 2,766,889 square kilometers

Capitol: Buenos Aires

Population: 32,901,234 (1992)

Official Language: Spanish

Major Religion: Roman Catholicism

Government: Republic

Monetary Unit: Peso

Chile — "The Rebellion of the Magical Rabbits" and "A Huge Black Umbrella"

Official Name: Republic of Chile

Area: 756,945 square kilometers

Capital: Santiago

Population: 13,528,945 (1992)

Official Language: Spanish

Major Religion: Roman Catholicism

Government: Republic

Monetary Unit: Peso

Where Angels Glide at Dawn *(cont.)*

Puerto Rico —"The Day We Went to See Snow" and "Fairy Tale"
Official Name: Commonwealth of Puerto Rico
Area: 9,104 square kilometers
Capital: San Juan
Population: 3,522,520 (1990)
Official Languages: Spanish and English
Major Religion: Christianity
Government: (ongoing debate) Commonwealth (favored by the Popular Democratic Party), Statehood (favored by the New Progressive Party), or Independence Political Factions (favored by the Independence Party)
Monetary Unit: Peso

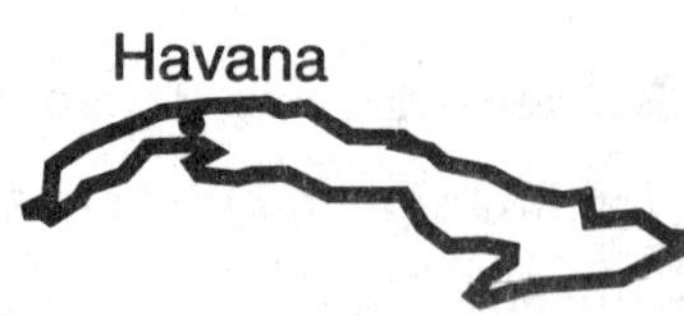

Cuba — "With My Eyes Closed"
Official Name: Republic of Cuba
Area: 114,524 square kilometers
Capital: Havana
Population: 10,846,821 (1992)
Official Language: Spanish
Major Religion: Roman Catholicism
Government: Communist one-party state
Monetary Unit: Cuban peso

Panama — "The Cave"
Official Name: Republic of Panama
Area: 77,082 square kilometers
Capital: Panama City
Population: 2,529,902 (1992)
Official Language: Spanish
Major Religion: Roman Catholicism
Government: Republic
Monetary Unit: Balboa

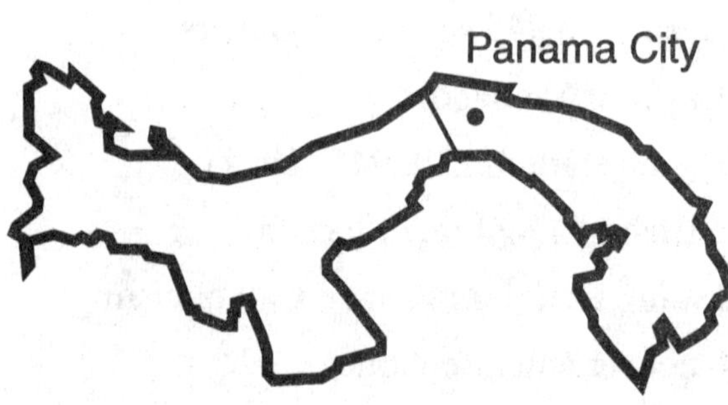

Where Angels Glide at Dawn (cont.)

Mexico — "Paleton and the Musical Elephant"
Official Name: United Mexican States
Area: 1,958,201 square kilometers
Capital: Mexico City
Population: 92,380,721 (1992)
Official Language: Spanish
Major Religion: Roman Catholicism
Government: Republic
Monetary Unit: Peso

El Salvador — "A Clown's Story"
Official Name: Republic of El Salvador
Area: 21,040 square kilometers
Capital: San Salvador
Population: 5,574,279 (1992)
Official Language: Spanish
Major Religion: Roman Catholicism
Government: Republic
Monetary Unit: Colon

Peru — "Tarma"
Official Name: Republic of Peru
Area: 1,285,216 square kilometers
Capital: Lima
Population: 22,889,000 (1993)
Official Languages: Spanish and Quechua
Major Religion: Roman Catholicism
Government: Republic
Monetary Unit: Nuevo Sol

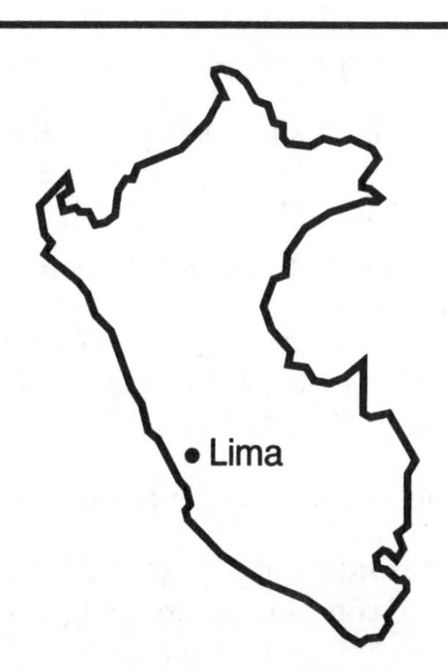

Where Angels Glide at Dawn *(cont.)*

Connecting Activities:

"The Bear's Speech"

- Have students locate Argentina on the South America map on page 138.

- This story is very abstract. The "bear" is not really a bear; instead, it represents something else. Ask students what they think the bear really is.

"The Rebellion of the Magical Rabbits"

- Have students locate Chile on the South America map on page 138.

- Have students discuss why the wolves want all the rabbits destroyed.

- Whenever the monkey takes a photograph of the wolf a bunny appears in the picture. At first it is just a hidden ear or tail, but eventually it is the entire bunny. Have students draw a picture of the wolf with a bunny ear hidden somewhere in the picture.

- Ask students to predict what eventually will happen to the wolf.

"The Day We Went to See Snow"

- Have students locate Puerto Rico on the Central America map located on page 47.

- Have students trace the journey the family makes to see the snow. First have them draw maps of Puerto Rico, then with brightly colored pens or markers, have them trace the journey from Bayamon to Santurce to Condado to San Juan, their final destination.

- The children really become anxious upon being in the car for such a long ride. Have students brainstorm a list of enjoyable activities that can be done on long car trips.

- The mayor brings the snow to San Juan for everyone to enjoy. Have students write speeches for the mayor to give to the people explaining why she decided to bring snow to them.

- Have students discuss in small groups their opinions of the parents in the story.

"With My Eyes Closed"

- Have students locate Cuba on the Central America map on a map.

- The young girl is upset to see some boys torturing a rat. Ask students whether they would consider this cruelty to animals. Then, in small groups, have them write laws that prohibit cruelty to animals and specify what "cruelty" means.

- Have students discuss why the girl found the street beggars running a candy store.

- The young girl says that the story of her accident is not a lie. However, it does seem rather odd. Have students write stories describing what they think really happened.

Where Angels Glide at Dawn (cont.)

"The Cave"

- Have students locate Panama on the Central America map on page 47.

- Have students write stories to explain what really happened to Anita in "the cave."

- As a class, discuss why cats are so prominent in all the stories in the book.

"Paleton and the Musical Elephant"

- Have students locate Mexico on the North America map located on page 124.

- Paleton collects expensive items. Have students share what they collect or would like to collect.

- Have students predict what will happen to Paleton's treasures after he is sent to jail.

- Have students draw pictures of the elephant and a piano.

"A Clown's Story"

- Have students locate El Salvador on the Central America map on page 47.

- Have students make large advertisements for Cachirulo's circus act.

- Cachirulo talks about how he has a smile on even though he is sad inside. Have students write about times when they pretended they were happy when they really were upset about something.

- Cachirulo was a clown when his country was in the midst of a civil war. Now, unfortunately, he has lost his circus. Have students predict what Cachirulo will do with his life.

Where Angels Glide at Dawn (cont.)

"Tarma"

- Have students locate Peru on the South America map on page 138.

- Have students research the Holy Week holiday celebrated in Peru.

- As part of the celebration the children picked flowers to decorate the streets. Have students make tissue flowers to cover a bulletin board.

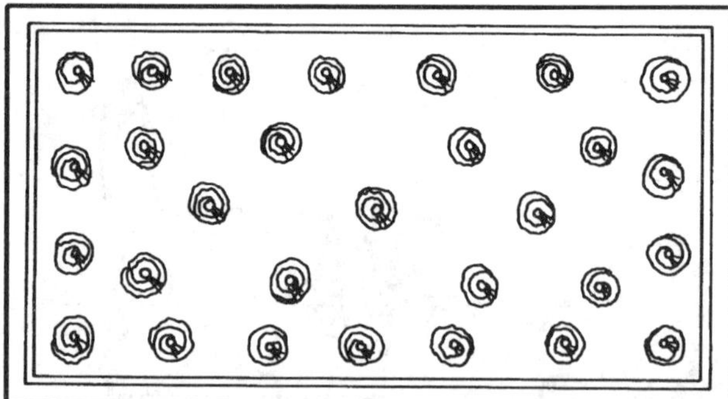

"Fairy Tale"

- Have students locate Puerto Rico on a map.

- Monica's mother does not like her to study because she thinks it is a waste of time. She wants Monica to work in a beauty shop because the family needs money. Monica's father, however, wants her to study and go to college. Have students write position essays stating with which parent they agree and why.

- Monica's mother tells Monica's father that he is like Don Quixote. Have students research who Don Quixote is. Then have them discuss whether being like Don Quixote is a compliment or insult.

- Monica is interested in college. Have students fill out college applications as if they were Monica. They can be given the application located on page 131 of this book. For some of the questions they will have to use their imaginations and answer based on what they know about Monica from reading the story.

- Monica's grandmother tells frightening stories to the children at night. Have students write scary stories that the grandmother could tell.

- Monica is excited that her parents decided to let her go to Puerto Rico for her vacation. Have students discuss where they would choose to go for vacation and why.

"A Huge Black Umbrella"

- Have students locate Chile on the South America map on page 138.

- Have students predict to whom Delfina has been writing all these years.

- Delfina is one of the few survivors of the Chilean earthquake. Have students research earthquakes that have occurred in Chile. Then have them write brief reports of their findings including the likelihood of there being another earthquake in Chile.

College Entrance Application

Fill out this application as if you are Monica. You will have to make up some of the answers because not all the information is included in the story. Do your best to answer based on what you do know about Monica.

Applicant's Full Name ____

Age ____

Date of Birth ____

Address ____

____

High School Attended ____

Grade Point Average ____

List any academic honors received in high school. ________________________

____

List any extracurricular activities. ___________________________________

____

High School Major ____

List any work experience. ____

____

Intended College Major ____

Full-time Student or Part-time Student? _________________________________

What will you do upon graduation from college? _________________________

____

____

Will you need financial assistance? ___________________________________

Explain your financial situation. ______________________________________

Secret of the Andes

Author: Ann Nolan Clark

Publisher: Penguin, New York, 1952. 130 pages

Summary: Cusi lives with Chuto high in the mountains of Peru. Cusi is happy living with Chuto but longs to find his real family. After some soul searching, Cusi realizes that although Chuto is not a blood relative, he is family.

Background Information on Peru:

Official Name: Republic of Peru

Area: 496,223 square miles

Capital: Lima

Population: 22,889,000 (1993)

Official Languages: Spanish and Quechua

Major Religion: Roman Catholicism

Government: Republic

Monetary Unit: New Sol

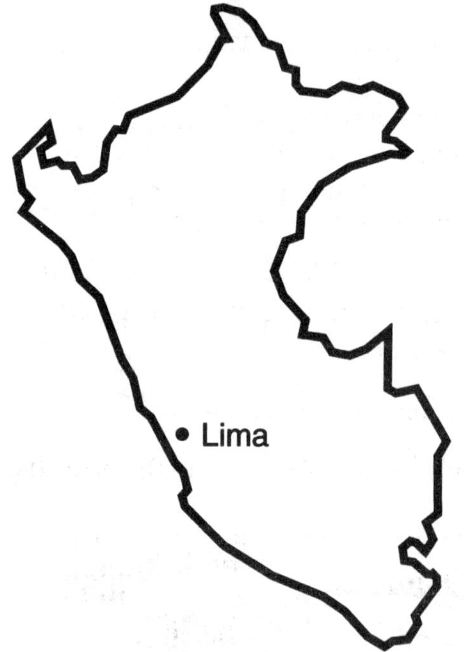

Connecting Activities:

(Chapters 1-2)

- Have students locate Peru on the South America map on page 138.

- Have students write essays describing what they think it would be like to never see people.

- Chuto makes the following statement, "Curiosity can leap the highest wall; an open gate is better." Have students respond to what this quote means.

- Cusi and Chuto are about to embark upon a journey. Cusi worries about his llama Misti missing him. Ask students whether they think it is possible for an animal to miss someone.

- The minstrel knows many songs. He sings about the stars, about the Pleiades guarding the newly planted seeds, about Venus, and about the Milky Way. Have students write a song about any of these topics.

Secret of the Andes (cont.)

- In small groups, have students discuss why Cusi is suddenly allowed to go on the journey and to greet the sun.

- To Cusi and Chuto the sunrise is very important. They greet the sun with prayer every day. Assign students to watch a sunrise and write descriptive essays about what they saw and what the experience was like.

- Cusi has no information about his real parents. Have students predict what happened to his parents, then write stories about it.

(Chapters 3-5)

- Have students find Cuzco and Lima on the South America map located on page 138.

- It is mentioned many times in the story about the Spaniards conquering the Incas. Have students write research reports about this topic. It will help them to better understand the story.

- Chuto is weaving a mat for his journey with Cusi. Have students weave mats by following the directions below.

Materials: 2 pieces of large construction paper, scissors, glue

1. Cut the construction paper into ½ inch (1.3 cm) strips.

2. Weave the two colors together. Start with one color strip and glue the other color strips to it, laying them next to each other. Then, weave the original color strips through the second color that has been glued on.

3. Glue any loose strips in place.

4. You may wish to laminate these for the students.

- The minstrel plays panpipes. Challenge students to find out what a panpipe is and to draw a picture of one.

Secret of the Andes (cont.)

- Have students write essays predicting what Cusi thinks the journey will be like. The essays should be from Cusi's point of view.

- Cusi somehow knows the story about the ancient llamas, even though he has never been told. In small groups have students debate whether or not Cusi has some kind of special powers.

- Cusi has had no contact with people other than Chuto and the minstrel. Yet, he is about to embark upon a journey during which he will undoubtedly meet many new people. Have students write letters of advice to Cusi telling him what they think he should know about people in general.

- Have students discuss why Chuto seems hesitant to go on their journey.

- The trail that Chuto and Cusi take is described in detail in the book, so is the bridge they have to cross. Have students draw pictures of either of these places based on the descriptions in the book.

- Cusi is very scared as he goes across the shaky bridge. Have students write about times they were really afraid of something, yet overcame their fears.

(Chapters 6-8)

- Challenge students to find out what causes landslides in Peru and whether or not landslides are a common occurrence there.

- When Chuto and Cusi meet the old Indian man he inquires about "the other one." Chuto responds by saying that "death has no returning." Have students discuss and then respond in writing to the exchange between these two men.

- We do not know the story of Cusi's past. We only know that now he is in Chuto's care. Have students write the prequel to the story. How did Cusi end up with Chuto? What happened to his parents?

- Cusi finds many things fascinating about the outside world. Take a class vote to see what students think Cusi finds to be the most interesting on his journey.

- Cusi longs to find his family. Yet, he has spent his life with Chuto. Does this make them a family? Have students respond to this question. Then ask them what they think makes a real "family."

Secret of the Andes (cont.)

(Chapters 9-11)

- In small groups, have students predict who they think Amauta is and what he has been sent to teach Cusi.

- Cusi is learning all about the history of the Incas. Have students research the history of the Incas and write a report of what they have learned.

- Cusi is learning well from Amauta. Challenge students to make report cards for Cusi. They can use the categories of things Amauta set out for him to learn. Then have students grade Cusi based on what they think Amauta would give him.

- Have students write essays describing from Cusi's point of view what he thinks his real family will be like.

- Have students predict whether or not they think Cusi will ever return to Chuto.

(Chapters 12-14)

- Cusi and Chuto would have great difficulty traveling without their llamas. Have the class make a mural of the mountains where Cusi and Chuto live. Then have them color and cut out the llama pattern on page 136. Each student can place his/her llama somewhere on the mural.

- Cusi is told to "follow his heart." Challenge students to describe what this means.

(Chapters 15-17)

- The family that chooses Cusi has a great time learning their fortunes. Allow students to write two different fortunes. Then allow each student to pick a fortune.

- Have students write good-bye notes from Cusi to the family that took him in, explaining why he has to leave.

- Now that Cusi has been out on his own, he realizes that Chuto is his family. Ask students whether they think this realization would have happened if Cusi had not been allowed to journey on his own.

Llama Pattern

Color this llama pattern, and then cut it out to be placed on the class mural.

South America Bibliography

Alexander, Ellen. *Llama and the Great Flood: A Folktale from Peru.* (Crowell, 1989)

Ancona, George. *Turtle Watch.* (Macmillan, 1987)

Barbot, Daniel. *A Bicycle for Rosaura.* (Miller, 1991)

Brusca, Maria Christina. *On the Pampas.* (Holt, 1991)

Castaneda, Omar. *Among the Volcanoes.* (Lodestar, 1991)

Charles, Donald. *Chancay and the Secret of Fire.* (Putnam, 1992)

Cohen, Miriam. *Born to Dance Samba.* (Harper & Row, 1984)

Cowcher, Helen. *Rain Forests.* (Farrar, Straus, & Giroux, 1988)

Dorros, Arthur. *Tonight Is Carnival.* (Dutton, 1991)

Flora. *Feathers Like a Rainbow: An Amazon Indian Tale.* (Harper & Row, 1989)

George, Jean Craighead. *One Day in the Tropical Rain.* (Crowell, 1990)

Huntley, Beth. *Amazon Adventure.* (Gareth Stevens Inc., 1989)

Jenkins, Lyll Becerra de. *The Honorable Prison.* (Dutton, 1988)

Moeri, Louise. *The Forty-Third War.* (Houghton Mifflin, 1989)

Wisniewski, David. *Rain Player.* (Houghton Mifflin, 1991)

Map of South America

Rainbow Bird

Author: Eric Maddern

Illustrator: Adrienne Kennaway

Publisher: Little, Brown, Boston, 1993. 24 pages

Summary: This aboriginal folk tale is about a dragon that wants to keep all the fire to himself.

Background Information on Australia:

Official Name: Commonwealth of Australia

Area: 7,682,300 square kilometers

Capital: Canberra

Population: 17,000,000 (1993)

Official Language: English

Major Religions: Protestantism and Roman Catholicism

Government: Federal Parliamentary State

Monetary Unit: Australian Dollar

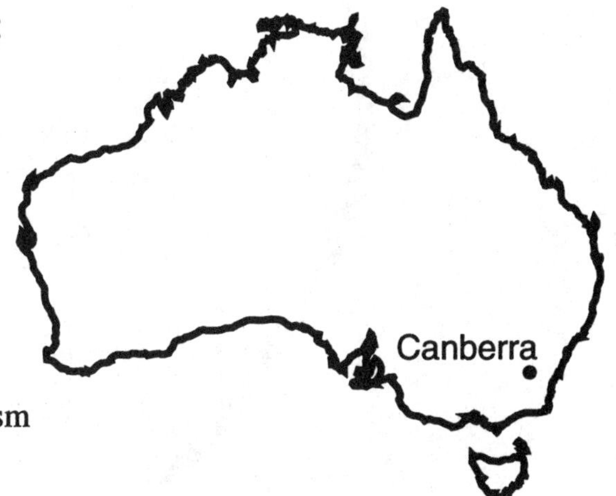

Connecting Activities:

- Have students locate Australia on the South Pacific map located on page 143.

- Have students draw pictures of crocodiles with fire coming out of their mouths. To make the picture more dramatic, allow students to use red and orange colored cellophane paper for the fire.

- Allow students to make beautiful rainbow birds. They can use the patterns located on pages 140 and 141.

- Have students write endings to the story and include explanations for why the crocodile now has to stay in the water.

- Have students write thank-you letters to rainbow bird from any of the animals or people who may have benefited from the use of fire.

- Allow students to be very creative and write their own folk tales explaining the origin of fire.

Rainbow Bird Patterns

Use the patterns below and on the next page to create your own rainbow bird. Remember to make the feathers as colorful as possible.

Rainbow Bird Patterns (cont.)

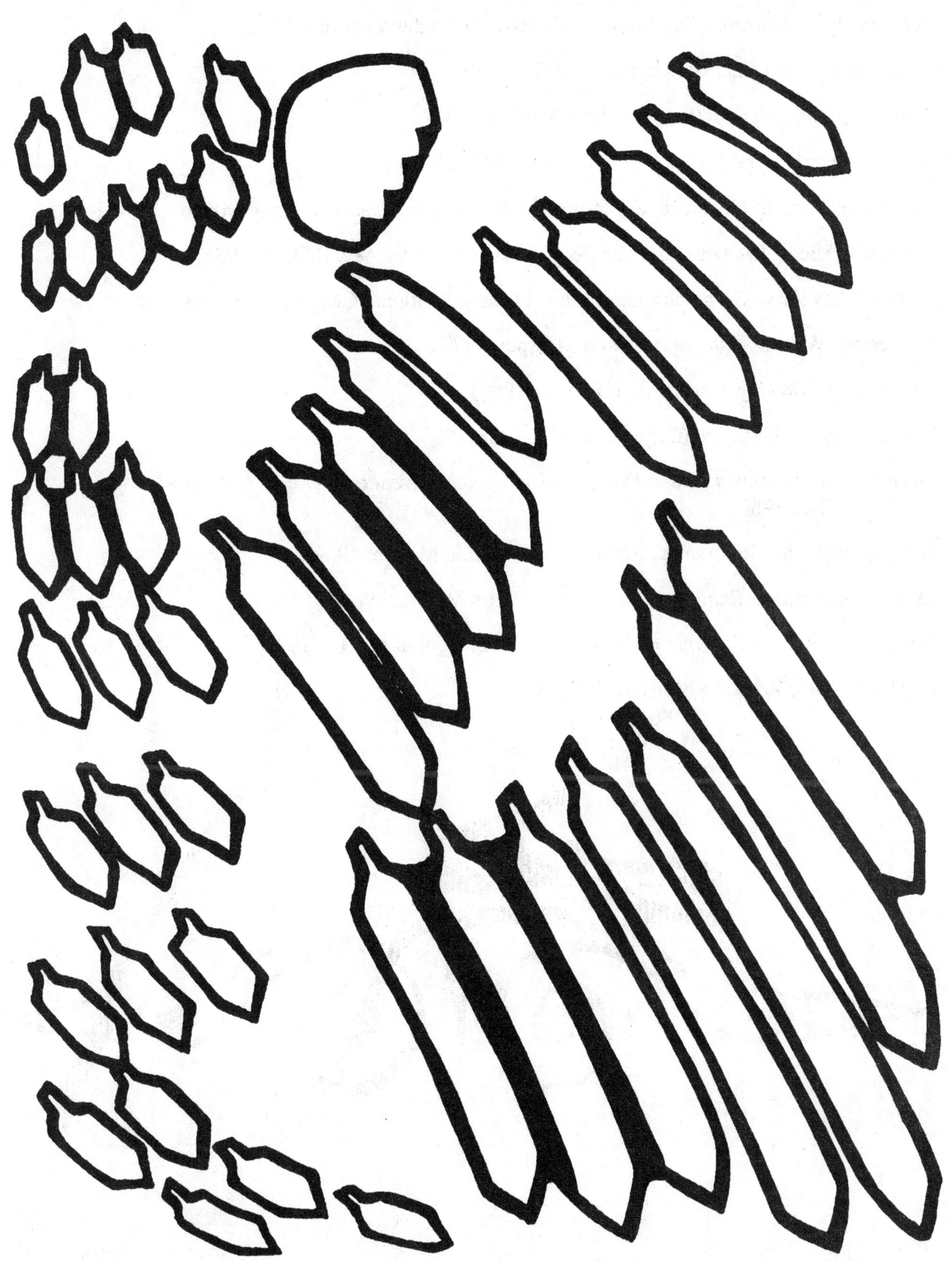

South Pacific Bibliography

Base, Graeme. *My Grandma Lived in Gooligulch.* (Australian Book Service, 1988)

Burt, Jocelyn. *Australia: The Unique Continent.* (Houghton Mifflin, 1991)

Carr, Roger. *The Clinker.* (Houghton Mifflin, 1989)

DeHamel, Joan. *Hemi's Pet.* (Houghton Mifflin, 1987)

Dunlop, Beverly. *The Poetry Girl.* (Houghton Mifflin, 1989)

Gascoigne, Toss, Jo Goodman, & Margot Tyrell. *Dream Time.* (Houghton Mifflin, 1991)

Gilbreath, Alice. *The Great Barrier Reef: A Treasure in the Sea.* (Dillon, 1986)

Harrell, Mary Ann. *Surprising Lands Down Under.* (National Geographic Society, 1990)

Henderson, W.F. *Looking at Australia.* (Harper, 1977)

Loh, Morag. *Tucking Mommy In.* (Orchard, 1988)

Luis, Nicholas. *Australia.* (Cagogan Books, 1988)

McGovern, Ann. *Down Under, Down Under: Diving Adventures on the Great Barrier Reef.* (Macmillan, 1989)

Savage, Deborah. *Flight of the Albatross.* (Houghton Mifflin, 1989)

Savage, Deborah. *A Rumour of Otters.* (Houghton Mifflin, 1986)

Savage, Deborah. *A Stranger Calls Me Home.* (Houghton Mifflin, 1992)

Ward, Glenyse. *Wandering Girl.* (Holt, 1991)

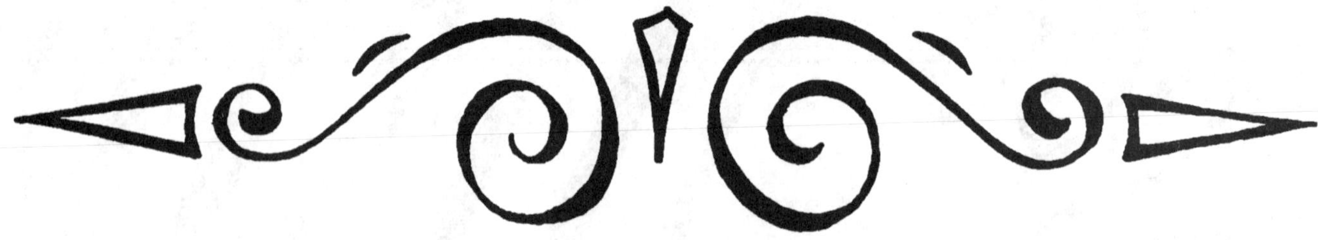

Map of the South Pacific

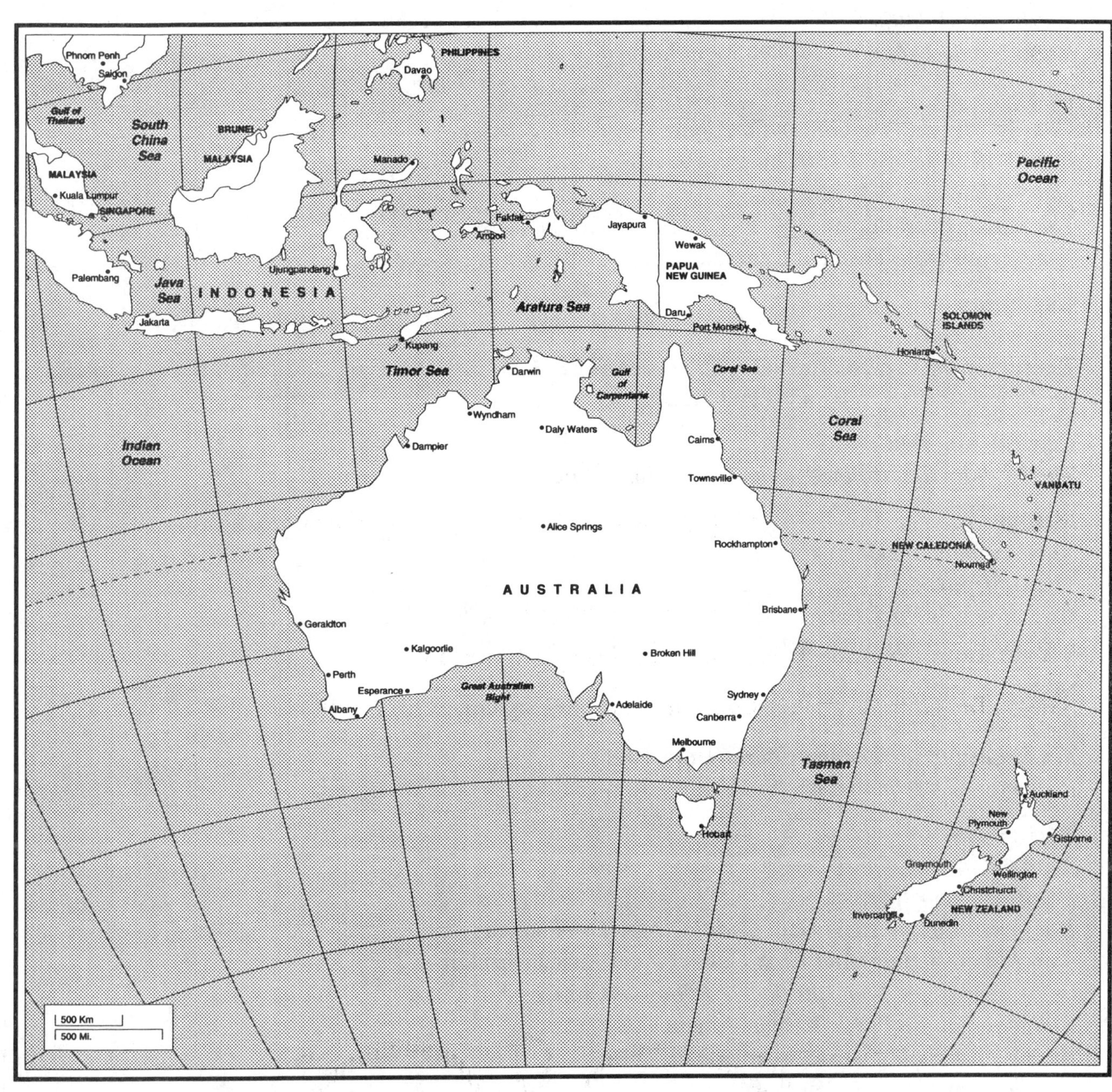

Index of Cultures